BOY ON A BICYCLE

Conan Kennedy

Going Home?

S MOKE ROSE FROM HIS CIGARETTE. I noticed that from a distance. And decided that he was being thoughtful, sitting there on the bench. But maybe he wasn't, maybe it was just that the sight of someone sitting alone and smoking a cigarette gives rise to that impression.

"You took your time" he said as I cycled up.

"It's bloody far on a bike" I told him.

I parked the machine, upright, pedal against the kerb in traditional manner. People don't do that anymore. And it'd be unwise, very. These days a bike needs to be locked securely to some immovable item of street furniture. A bike left casual against a kerb these days? Say goodbye. Sayonara. Goodnight Vienna, all that.

"It's the same distance on a bike as in a car," my father said, "and don't say bloody. Your mother doesn't like it."

"May be the same *distance*…" I muttered, and sat down beside him.

And so we sat there for a while. Myself tired from the ride and he thoughtful with his cigarette. Thoughtful or whatever that mood he was in, he was alone with his cigarette anyway. I didn't smoke. But then I

BOY ON A BICYCLE

First published in 2012 by
Morrigan New Century
Killala, Co. Mayo, Ireland

morriganbooks@gmail.com

A CIP catalogue record for this work is available
from The British Library.

ISBN 978-0-907677-46-8
Cover (colour) photographs by John D Cully.
Photographs elsewhere are 1960's views in public domain.

Design and origination by
Hayes Design, St Leonards on Sea, Sussex, England.

Printed in England by MPG Biddles, Kings Lynn, Norfolk.

was only fourteen, going on fifteen. Though come to think of it, even when I was older and did smoke he never once offered me a cigarette. And he lived to ninety two. Never once offered. Have a cigarette? No. Never. Not once. Maybe he didn't approve. Which was strange, because he worked as a travelling salesman for a cigarette company. Not that approval mattered one way or the other...because when older I just swiped his samples from the cupboard anyway. And thus as a teenager I always had cigarettes. Which made me popular among the boys I knew. Yes I was nearly going to write *among my friends* just there, but decided that'd be stretching it a bit.

My father and I sat there on the bench in Shankill with our backs to the Catholic Church. A position that we both more or less maintained throughout our lives. He for the simple reason that he was a Protestant and I, a Roman Catholic, for more complex reasons of faith and idealogy. Had he not married a Catholic I too would have been a Protestant. More relaxing in some ways, or so I sometimes reckon...sometimes reckon not. Being a writer bad enough, and an Irish writer worse, not sure at all how I would've handled that triple whammy of being a Protestant Irish writer.

He'd bought me the bike in Kilmacanogue, in the garage there which had a little shop attached. One of his customers, as he described them. Being a travelling salesman for a cigarette company was a popular calling among those customers. And deals and favours were exchanged, and I suppose he likely got a few bob off the price of the bike. He once explained to me why cigarette salesman were very popular among shopkeepers...it was because of the war.

"The war?"

"The war, before you were born. There was cigarette rationing. Shops tried to get as many cigarettes in as they could." And he drifted his hand in the air. That sort of gesture translated as *under the counter*, or as *you know how it is yourself.*

"Your mother and I never went short of tea," he added. And no, they hadn't. In my dimmest memories I recalled biscuit boxes of tea hidden in backs of cupboards.

Left over from the war. Illicit rationed tea.

"But it's not the war now," I pointed out, "it's bloody years since the war."

"Yes but Irish shopkeepers are very conservative. They think there could be another war at any minute. Probably right. And don't say bloody, your mother doesn't like it."

"So it's just they want to keep in with cigarette salesmen?"

"Exactly, exactly."

And so he had bought the bike at the right price in Kilmacanogue and we had driven down there to collect. It turned out to be a plain black simple bike, and I'd probably been expecting something a bit more flash, but a bike was a bike. A Raleigh, it had dark green piping edging the black enamel. And the lower part of the rear mudguard was painted blinding white around the shiny red reflector.

"You like it?" he said.

"It's great," I told him, "I'm going to ride it home."

"I was thinking we'd put it in the boot."

"No I want to ride it, try it out."

He shrugged. My father wasn't interested in taking decisions. Familywise he left them to his wife. And as to the rest, he drifted. We arranged that he'd wait for me in Shankill, and we'd see how it was going from there. Because after all there was Killiney Hill ahead, and I might be tired of cycling. So off he drove and I followed on the bike. It wasn't a motorway then, but a fair old busy road enough. And cars whizzed by too close and I felt the first stirrings of that animosity between cyclist and motorist. Bastards, I thought. And heard my father say don't say bastards, your mother doesn't like it.

I cycled on.

Past those premises which are now the *Avoca Woollen Mills*, that fashionable pit stop for ladies who lunch, buy Ballymaloe cookbooks, and rarely cook. I don't know what the place was in those times. And didn't really care. Just cycled on, past all that land on the right which my family now owns, now *Brennanstown Riding School*. Well, here I use the term *my family* at its loosest, it being actually my sister who owns it. And I'm none too sure how *family* she considers me. Doubt I'm in the deeds. It hardly matters. Families come and go, as does ownership of land...and the land hardly cares so why should I?

I cycled on, and on. And reached a fork in the road, and a fork in the mind too. To veer left and go down through Bray or continue on the main road to Little Bray....decision? I decided on the route through Little Bray. Something about that road I always liked, and still do. Perhaps because it winds the river, and something ancient appeals. And one is on the trail of ancient journeys. Another thing, it has the air of the glory days of motoring. One expects an open topped tourer to come around the bend. Driver in goggles, his bobbed haired companion in a cloche hat. I've never actually seen that scene but I reckon it's somewhere in the senses. From pictures in old books, magazines. Whatever, I definitely sense all that on that particular piece of road. But that is now. Back then I neither sensed nor thought nor knew. Mysticism was at a low level.

Into Little Bray. I've always liked the concept of Little Bray. And actually as a child wondered why there wasn't a Little Dalkey, or a Little Dún Laoghaire. It just seemed appropriate to have a place, and then another but smaller place of the same name beside it. Young people have interesting minds, before they get gummed up by life and experience and rationality. Adulthood another word for early Alzheimers? No doubt.

Around Sunnybank next. Sunnybank which I didn't know then should more correctly be called Bloody Bank. Its proper name. Bloody Bank because of old battles and slaughter. Mountainy tribes coming across the Dargle to rape and pillage...Dubliners trying to stop them. What else is new? Apart from the name of the place. Bloody Banks. Sensitive souls just changed the name.

Next the Solus water tower, black and white over there like the packaging of one of their light bulbs.

Clever in its imagery.

Ireland needed more of that back then.

And now we've gotten less.

But onwards, ever onwards.

After the Solus water tower the road changed in those times, and still changes now. It became and still does become more rural, old fashioned somehow. One definitely senses that golden age of motoring mentioned, the golden age of cycling too. Perhaps it's those huge old trees that do it. And that Crinken Church, like somewhere heart of England.

"They're not really Protestants in there," my father told me once.

"What do you mean, not really?"

"They're disconnected. They don't recognise the bishop."

"What do you mean they don't recognise the bishop?"

"His authority. It's complicated. We're the ancient Irish church you know, the Church of Ireland. And we're complicated."

"The Protestants split from the Catholics," I corrected, " Martin Luther."

"Not in Ireland. We were here first. The Pope sent people to take us over. We resisted. That's why we're still here. Not many of us though. When I was growing up a quarter of Dublin was protestant. Look at us now."

I did.

I pedalled on, past that big house *The Aske* where my uncle lived way back. Not that I knew that then, as boy on a bicycle, I merely cycled by. Past the cemetery which wasn't a cemetery in those days. Just fields, waiting for flesh as fields do. No need for that cemetery then. All the people buried there were still alive. Some hardly born. But the earth waiting for them. Ever so patient, the earth.

Onward, ever on. Past that housing estate where my sister lives right now. Not that she knew that back then, doing her Leaving in *The Holy Child Convent*. On into the village of Shankill. Up the hump to the railway bridge. And down again. And across to the bench beside the church where my father sat.

In different times, these different times he would be sitting almost opposite the nursing home where my mother was to die. Though he went before her, and never saw her there. But did he know, did he know back then as he sat there waiting maybe thoughtfully? Did he know that one day he might sit there as a ghost, thinking of her?

Hard to tell.

But it was there for him to know. As indeed all the future is. Life is much like going though IKEA, following that arrowed winding path. But there are hidden doors to circumvent that tedious arrowed path. Hidden in IKEA for the staff, and in life for the wise.

Neither of us particularly wise, my father and I sat there on that bench for a while, me getting my rest, him smoking. Then he stood up, dropped his cigarette, and stamped out the butt with his heel, twisting like it was alive and might escape. He asked me if we'd put the bike in the boot and drive the rest. I told him no, I might as well finish the journey. And he said please yourself, and drove away, a decision made for him. And I got back on the bike and cycled on. And near Ballybrack it was time for me to make another decision. Up Killiney Hill and down again? Or through Ballybrack Village and along Church Road and past Killiney Golf Club? Then up Ballinclea Road to Killiney Road and home?

One route was hillier and harder, but shorter.

The other flatter and easier, but longer.

The choice…hmmnn…one of those tricky ones.

Like Robert Frost I took the road less travelled, and not for the last time. Yes, I took the hillier. And yes, the reader tells me told you so, yes half way up Killiney Hill I regretted it, getting off to push. Ah well. Many times through life I have regretted the journey, and have gotten off to push. But still and all, on arrival in Killiney Village I was glad. And celebrated with an icecream from Rita's Shop. Big Rita, big big haired Rita. Her husband was a carpenter. Fell off scaffolding in the building of the *Holy Child Convent*. Got serious compo. Spent the rest of his life in the pub next door, *The Druid's Chair*.

Stories? Yes, I've got stories.

From Killiney Village it was all downhill from there on in. Literally, in every direction. No matter which way chosen. It was impossible *not* to go downhill. Easy. Reckon in life you do get to that place, eventually.

And once there?

That phrase again…might as well finish the journey.

I got on the bike and freewheeled down.

Past the house where Séan Ó Faoláin lived. He was a writer, I remind the reader. And why? Because it's necessary to remind. Dead writers are dead in a much more complete manner than non-writers. Anyway, my father ran over Séan Ó Faoláin's dog and killed it. Right there outside that house. The incident was more or less my father's only connection to the world of literature.

I freewheeled on.

Past that big posh house whose teenage daughter had an affair with the conductor of the 59 bus. An affair that was regularly consummated in the bushes behind Killiney Village called *The Rocks*. Kind of apt name, in those circumstances. I just couldn't make this up. And how the bus kept leaving late and that's how it all came out in a scandal. No, her parents weren't that pleased. But of course all the other parents around Killiney were, mightily. The posh people in that posh house were generally considered to have lost the run of themselves.

Her name was? And she married?

You're kidding me, this is not that sort of book.

But stories? As mentioned, I've got them.

But I hadn't many then, boy on a bicycle. Back then I was just going home, or so I thought, going home. But of course I wasn't. I was fourteen going on fifteen. And I had a bike. And I was leaving.

Bogland

I WENT TO DONEGAL. Myself and the new bike. In fact the main reason I had the new bike at all was the fact that I was headed for Donegal. I needed a bike in Irish College. Or so said the instructions. And there were a lot of instructions. In two languages. But they strangely omitted to tell us to also bring food and blankets and a personal psychiatric advisor. We'd be needing them.

I went to Gortahork in Donegal with Philip Boucher Hayes. No, not the present day RTÉ journalist, but his father of the same name. We were schoolboys together and were off to learn Irish for a summer month. We'd come back native speakers, so many mini-Padraig Pearses, not to mention mini-Pearsettes.

It was a noble dream.

And we were part of that dream, and proud.

And also hoping to meet lots of mini-Pearsettes and get into, if not their knickers, at least their bras. In those days getting into the former was slightly more ambitious than the culture of the times allowed.

We gathered our hormones at Connolly Station. Still called Amiens Street then, it was much the same as now. But smellier with steam and smoke from great rumbling engines. Quite dramatic really. To us Dublin suburban youths it was something like heading off on the Venice

Simplon. To the unknown, to an exotic place. And I suppose we were.

We were going to Bogland.

Gangs of us, fourteen, fifteen, that age. Each boy stood beside a bike. And mine stood out. I hadn't actually wanted it to stand out. Because by extension that would lead to myself standing out, and teenage boys like to fit in. It's the gang culture. But my father had a notion. The bike was a month or so old but he didn't get to be a cigarette salesman for forty years without planning ahead. And he had saved the bike-shaped cardboard factory wrapping that the bike originally had in Kilmacanogue, saved it for just this occasion. This was necessary, very necessary. Or so he said. Because the bike would be thrown in the guard's van and scratched and wrecked on the journey. Or so he said. So best to wrap it back up again.

That cardboard covered bike beside me on the platform made me look like a prick. Not to mention making me the subject of mockery and general derision. It was not a role I cherished, though in adulthood I've just had to come to terms with its continual re-emergence. But I suppose any psychological trauma wasn't my father's concern. He'd had a cold shower upbringing, a be-a-man-the-natives-are-restless-upbringing. And his interest was in protecting his investment. Buying me another bike was not on his agenda. One son, one bike. A sacred mantra to him, much like one man, one vote. Well, much like one man one vote would be to the majority of people. He himself wasn't too keen on that notion. Particularly if it involved Roman Catholics.

The bike was thrown into the guard's van and off we set. The journey took us first to Derry city, thence Letterkenny, and then from there to Gortahork. Somewhere half way along the journey the boys got tired of taking the piss out of me, so that was ok. And there were lots of girls on the train, from Muckross College. So that was better. Their destination was the same as ours. Learning Irish. And they all looked very pretty. Even the ugly ones, desirable. But I decided to save those ones for later and start at the top, working myself downwards to the natural level appropriate to my personal charm and attractiveness.

I struck up conversation with a very pretty ponytailed blonde.

Looking back now there seems to have been several pony tailed blondes in my story of those times.. Maybe they were just a type, common in those days. Olivia Newton John as in the movie *Saturday Night Fever* reminds me of those girls. If perhaps a slightly older version.

This particular PTB (pony tailed blonde) was from the Trees Road in Mount Merrion. Or so she told me, and why would she lie? I didn't know anything about Mount Merrion, it was beyond bicycle range. I actually thought Mount Merrion people were quite exotic. Somehow less primitive than us Dún Laoghaire folks. They had bowling alleys and shopping centres. We had the sea. And Killiney Hill. And the sea.

Now let's get serious. Gortahork in those days was neither Dún Laoghaire nor Mount Merrion. It was a squalid moonscape of dereliction and decay. Of weedy thatch and thin lipped women, disappointed men. But they did speak Irish, and whether that was connected with the state of the place is probably both here and there. The Irish language has no word for litter.

So, now that my gaeilgeoir daughter has disowned me, I will move right on.

On arrival we were taken to a hall, it was bleak. With the atmosphere and design standards of a concentration camp processing facility. Functional. There we were divided into groups, as if some for gassing, others for hard work. Well, the boys were processed in this manner. The girls had somehow vanished by then, hustled off elsewhere by hatchet faced old bats. There were a lot of hatchet faced old bats around. They spoke Irish. A later wisdom tells me now that they probably farted in Irish...through those square backsides they hid in tweedy skirts.

I have died and gone to hell, I decided.

I hadn't.

I had gone to Bogland.

Guided by a mentor on a bike, a group of six of us cycled off into the hills. This was an improvement because those were the days before all that monstrous Donegal planning corruption and everything was still very picturesque. Around us were mountains and, yes, bogland, but it was picturesque. And the landscape was marred by few enough bungalows, just dotted with traditional cottages mostly. We were those kids in John Hinde postcards. I wished I'd worn a red jumper. It was all quite nice. I felt aesthetic emotions rising.

It wasn't to last.

At the bottom of a lane the mentor stroke guide stopped, and pointed up a track. You lot up there, he said, the *bean a tí* is expecting you. Well he didn't actually say those alien words, but we supposed that to be the gist of his Irish language instructions. And then he turned his bike and his back and cycled away towards Gortahork, towards a life I could write in an easy paragraph.

A student teacher then, this was his summer holiday. Handy for a few bob. Yes he did eventually become principal of a Christian Brothers school in a Dublin suburb. Married. A childhood sweetheart? Probably. Had three children. Died. And yes there's probably more, much more, certainly more, but I don't have time nor space nor words for every life that touches me. Barely enough time nor space nor words for my own.

The mentor left and we were alone. And it was getting dark.

But not so dark that we couldn't see a ditch beside the lane. And in that ditch a running stream of water, red water. Hey lookit the water, one of our number said, it's red. It was. We looked at it. Hey lookit that donkey, another of our number said. We looked at the donkey. It looked at us. That was about it, donkey wise. We set off up the track. The surface was very stony. We're going to get punctures coming down here someone said. Probably the same boy who had pointed out the donkey. Any group of six includes that someone.

The stony surface was shaped like the letter W, in that there were two deep ruts on either side of a mound in the middle. Some of us walked in one V of the W, the others in the other. I walked in the V at the side of the road that was next the ditch. And I noted as we climbed the hill that the water in the ditch got redder and redder. I didn't like that, I didn't like it at all. It was a sign! And the sun was going down.

We arrived, and mostly wished we hadn't.

12

The cottage was long with many doors and more windows, small windows that weren't going to say much until they knew you better. I noted at one end of the cottage how the windows were not glass, but slats of wood, as if someone had broken up a pallet and nailed bits there. They had, of course, as I was to learn later, much of Donegal's traditional architecture involved the use of old pallets.

Towards that end of the cottage there was a man and a boy. The boy was at the door, the man sat outside. Something was going on. We watched. The boy slung a sheep out towards the man, and the man cut its throat. And blood gushed out and flowed across the yard towards that ditch we had noted coming up. They were slaughtering sheep. And there was a pile of them dead against the wall of the cottage.

"Guess we'll be eating sheep," said the wit of our group. Who was Philip Boucher Hayes, father of the RTÉ journalist of the same name.

We went to the central door of the cottage. It stood between windows that had glass and evidence of light within.

"What do you boys want? said the *bean a tí*, in English. She wore a housecoat. I'd never seen a housecoat. Sexy it wasn't. But I suppose they were useful in areas where contraception was difficult to obtain.

"We've come to stay, we're from the College."

"Well I told them I could only take two, three at most. I've only two beds. My sister's over from Luton."

"But where will we go?" we asked.

It was dark, darker. The old man slaughtering sheep now seemed to be squeezing green liquidy stuff out of intestines. It mixed with the blood at his feet. They make sausages out of that, said the boy who had pointed out the donkey. The boy who prophesised punctures.

"Maybe we'll be having sausages," said Philip Boucher Hayes.

"Where will we go?" we asked again.

"Oh for fuck's sake come in, I'll sort it in the morning" said the *bean a tí*.

We went in. There was a hen walking round the kitchen floor. We looked at the hen. The hen looked at us. That was about it, hen wise.

"Would you like some sandwiches?" asked the *bean a tí*.

"What are they?" someone asked.

"Slices of bread with something in the middle" said another boy.

"They're sandwiches," said the *bean a tí*, "sandwiches."

"I mean what's in them ?" said the boy. And added "I like ham."

"Well you're not getting ham sandwiches here," said the *bean a tí*, "it's tomatoes. We have a greenhouse. A tomato greenhouse."

"Have you any cheese sandwiches?"

"We've tomato sandwiches."

"That'd be very nice," I said. "*Go raibh maith agat.*"

"*Ceart go leor*" said the *bean a tí*.

I'm a native speaker already, I thought.

She divided us up. The beds were actually big double beds, so there was three of us in each. Philip Boucher Hayes was one of the boys in mine. He told us ghost stories late into the night. The next day we were all divided up, and he went to another cottage. And I didn't really see him again, we were never particular friends. I don't think I liked him much, he and his family had a tiff about themselves. But who I liked and who liked me are facts as meaningful as the falling of a single leaf in a single year, a single year of…oh God must be forty.

Forty years went by and my mother had dementia now. But she also had a lot of money, so she had a carer. Lots of carers, a rotation of carers. And one morning my mother and I and one particular carer sat around the table in my mother's dining room. And I sat precisely where I used sit at Christmas dinners long years ago, my grandmother to one side, my Aunt Polly to the other. Their chairs were empty now.

I sat in the chair that was always my chair because from there I could help my mother with the serving, moving dishes back and forth. And I suppose I sat there from habit now. Just as from habit my mother sat at the head of the table where she had always sat. In authority. But now she didn't quite know who she was. And complained that she found it difficult, remembering, things. I told her yet again she'd had a fall, she'd fallen down the stairs, fractured her skull and that had caused confusion.

14

But I didn't tell her she had brain damage from the fall, and was never going to get better. And then she asked me "why, why did you let me fall down the stairs?"

Yes, I had long realised she thought she was a little girl, and that I was her father. And it was a cheerless realisation. So I shrugged at her and smiled, and she smiled too, forgetting that she'd asked a question, and questions came with answers. I looked at my fingers on the mahogany table, and remembered setting the places for those family Christmas dinners. We'd come from old decency and had silver and good glass. Pointy silver grapefruit spoons with one serrated edge, that sort of heirloom. One just has to be born to it really. No gentleman buys his own furniture, all that. Sorting out cutlery and glass and silver centrepieces and setting that table had been my job. I set a good table to this day. Not that I know why I was given the task as a teenager, I having five sisters. But I suppose they had other jobs. Prettying themselves for the party, and that. The younger ones wore velvet dresses with detachable linen collars. Queen Elizabeth was on the throne across the water, Queen Elizabeth the Second. But that Christmas table was more reminiscent of the First.

The carer and I chit chatted. An older woman, she wasn't the pretty busty young one I liked so I didn't flirt. Just chatted. My mother interjecting with inconsequential remarks. I said yes Mum. The carer said yes Mrs Kennedy. And we went on with the talk. And then my mother stood up and wandered off. Is she ok, I asked the carer? She's ok, she assured. And soon we saw her out there in the garden, ok, pottering, looking at plants. She had been something of a gardener. I doubt she knew their names now. Or even what plants actually were in the scheme of God's creation.

"It's hard for the family," the carer said.

I agreed. But that was about all there was to say about the matter so we continued to talk of other things. Gossippy things. She knew I was in the writing business and told me that her son-in-law was the journalist Philip Boucher Hayes. And I said oh, it's a small world. Because it was. Because I went to Bogland with another Philip Boucher Hayes. And I remembered.

That pretty Muckross girl on the train?

Didn't get next to near her in the amorous stakes. But worked my way down to a plainer and more suitable version. We lay behind a turf stack, the rest is history. Well, it's history if history be betrayal. Because in the years or so to come I'd see her at Dublin dances, and more or less ignored her. Because by then I'd worked my way higher up the food chain to prettier girls. I can still see her looking at me, across those crowded halls where the *Greenbeats* played. And other bands with names like *Bees Make Honey* and musicians with names like Deke O'Brian and Gerry Cott. I danced in those places and she did too. And now I feel bad for ignoring her. But then a man feels bad for lots of things. And I try to console myself that I was only a boy on a bicycle then, and not the fine rounded individual of grace and culture that I soon became. It offers no consolation. But rather desolation for a lost friendship, a lost sharing.

And Philip Boucher Hayes, father of the journalist of the same name?

Decades after Bogland I met him at the urinals in the *Bailey Pub* in Duke Street. Life hadn't been great to him, by appearances. But he still had that arrogant tiff about himself. It's a family thing. And he responded to my conversation with ascerbic remarks. Ascerbic to the point of dismissive, even contemptuous. Nothing I said impinged on his scheme of things. So outside the jacks we parted, he in one direction, I in the other. And the crowded bar swallowed us up in that slosh of laughters and conversations. Like we were items on a shore, washed by an incoming tide. And that was the same night an old man in a homburg hat came up to myself and my companions. An old Jewish man. He had a bunch of paintings under his arm, selling them. And we looked at them. They were cheap, but we were cheaper and didn't buy. Pity really. It was Harry Kernoff.

The years passed. My mother fell down the stairs. And I was writing in the *Irish Times*. And I had just written an article about an old school rugby photograph I had. And then my mother's carer said her son-in-law's father was in that photo, and would it be possible to get him a copy?

It was, and I did. And one Philip Boucher Hayes sent the photo to another Philip Boucher Hayes in England. The son to the father. And then very shortly after that the father died. Yes I have noticed that. Sometimes I meet or have vague renewed connection to people I knew long ago. For no reason, they come out of the blue, in conversation or coincidence. And then they die. As if their reappearance was their saying goodbye.

And it probably is.

S**HE TOLD ME** that she had a twin once. And that the twin was very beautiful, but she died young. And now there was only herself, and she wasn't beautiful, she was quite plain really.

"Do you think I'm plain?" Cathy asked me.

What a question to ask a fifteen year old boy !

A boy who was there under orders.

"You should visit your aunt," my mother had told me, "she's all alone in this world."

"I don't want to visit her, she's weird."

"You must, it's your duty. One day you too will be all alone in the world. And you'll want your nephews and nieces to visit you."

"Why will I be all alone in the world?" I asked.

"Because you have that about you," my mother told me.

"What have I got about me?"

"Aloneness. Now get on your bike and visit Aunt Cathy."

She was actually my great aunt. And she lived in Dungar Terrace down in Dún Laoghaire. And she didn't live alone at all, she lived with her brother Bob. But I suppose he had his own life and interests and that was what my mother meant. To all intents and purposes my Great Aunt Cathy lived alone.

My mother couldn't make her mind up without dragging other minds along in the same direction, so I had no choice. She had made her mind up. I got on my bike and cycled down to Dún Laoghaire. Via the Metals route. Albert Road to Metals, Metals to Corrig Road. I had many potential routes to Dún Laoghaire. And I varied them, depending on the mood. These differing routes actually took more or less the same time, expended the same energy…but it was a mood thing. And the mood today was along the Metals and up Corrig Road. And from there down Northumberland Avenue to the town. I sense that last bit is a one way these days, one way in the other direction. Not that that would make a blind bit of difference to a cyclist either then or now.

Dungar Terrace is short and narrow. And if it were a person I reckon it'd be likewise, it has that thing about it. Inward looking. And not entirely pleased with what it sees in there. All sense of hope and joy and fun seems drained. I cycled in…into the Dungar Terrace of the soul. All sense of hope and joy and fun left behind me in Northumberland Avenue. I prayed. In the sense of muttering *Oh God Oh God* as I approached number eight. Over and over, the final *Oh God* as I chained the bike to the railings. And as I did so my aunt sensed me in some way…maybe her familiar the cat went in and told her… and she opened the door and said "what if they steal the railings?"

"I'll get the bus home," I told her.

She smiled at that, and I realised once again that I actually liked Cathy, the witch in her. And I know now that I just hid that liking from myself by thinking her as weird. Boys aren't that seriously into witches. Until they become men, and are dealing with the woman thing. Both the woman thing in them, and in the wider female population.

Cathy didn't smile for long. If she'd been a weather system she wouldn't have been described as *settled*. More like *changeable*. With occasional wintry showers. She said come in and waved me into the hall, and that hall was very dark indeed. I remember nothing of the furniture, except that it was dark in the darkness. Darker than the darkness, looming like the hulks of sunken ships in some submarine environment. I remember no details. But I do remember the glow of a red lamp, a red bulbed votive lamp on the stairs. A red bulbed votive lamp whose filament was in the shape of a cross, and which flickered. Erratically. Not with the pulsing flicker of a modern digital clock radio, but with a shivery feeble flicker, as if signalling something in there that was just about clinging to life. This lamp stood in front of a statue. Five foot high, thereabouts. On the half landing of the stairs. A statue of The Sacred Heart, complete with external heart. And the external heart complete with a cross protruding from the super ventricular area.

Yes I remember all that.

The thing had given me the creeps as a younger kid. But now at fourteen I had come to terms with it. And just glanced up at it casually. And thought to myself *Oh God*. Which result was obviously the object of the whole manifestation anyway.

Cathy noticed my glance and remarked that the statue came from Drogheda, as she did herself. And I told her yes I know, you told me that before. And asked her what was Drogheda like. To expand the conversation. She smiled, and waved me towards the kitchen. Past those silent reception rooms reserved for more important visitors. I suspect that any such were few and far between. But the rooms were ready just in case. It's almost axiomatic, I have learned in later wisdom, almost axiomatic that rooms like that are neat and pristine in inverse proportion to the numbers of visitors. And such a learning is sad. But then I reckon most learning about life and people is to be avoided if sadness be a problem.

In the kitchen she told me about Drogheda. West Street where they lived. And how her father was in the drapery business. And her mother was a Carroll, connected to the cigarettes. And that her grandfather on her father's side was a sailor, a sea captain. Captain Michael McGovern. And she was actually born in his house on the quay by the river. And that house is still there, and there's a plaque on the wall with his name. And I should go and see it sometime.

"Why should I go and see it sometime?"

"Because then you'd know."

"What would I know?"

"More than you know now. You could go there on your bike. Make a day of it."

"A day? Drogheda's miles away. More like a week."

"Nonsense. You're young and strong. Bring a packed lunch. Picnic by the Boyne. We used picnic by the Boyne. When we were young. In Mornington by the river and watch the ships come in and out."

"Was it nice?"

"Picnic with my brother and sisters. My brother Bob. And my sister Mollie. She's your grandmother now."

"I know."

"And with my twin. She was very beautiful. But she died. Young." She nodded, and looked at me carefully. "Just at about your age," she added, not entirely cheeringly. Particularly as she did so she was looking me up and down, as if measuring for a coffin.

"That's sad," I said.

"Life is sad," said Cathy, "death sadder."

And then she shrugged such thoughts away and asked me what was I up to myself. So I told her something ridiculous and strange had happened, something that very morning.

"Oh good," she said, "I like ridiculous and strange, tell me about it. I'll put on the kettle."

So I told her.

My mother had *missed the meat*. In the sense that it was her habit to phone up Miss Bethune in Grimes' Butchers in Dalkey to order meat each day. They had their own abbatoir in the back. You'd see cattle go in on their last journey. That shop is still there, called Doyle's, but the abbatoir is gone. It's a beauty parlour now. Abbatoir converted to beauty parlour? But yes it's true…some things a writer just can't make up.

Miss Bethune was the clerical and financial functionary of the butchery. She sat in a little box in the shop like a laughing policeman at a funfair, taking orders on the phone. And the meat would be despatched by messenger boy bike to people's very door. You shop, we drop. But that morning my mother had phoned up late, and the boy had gone about his deliveries. She'd missed the meat! So she sent me to Dalkey to collect it instead, handing me a one pound note with the injunction "be careful of the change."

When my mother said be careful of the change she meant be careful of the change.

I cycled down to Dalkey, collected the meat, and paid Miss Bethune in her box. I suppose she was in her sixties, but what did I know? I was young, and only knew her name on the phone, and the occasional sight of her in that cashiers' box. But now I know some more. I am a genealogist, and an unusual name is a gift to the likes of me.

This woman whom I never knew was Catherine Bethune. She was daughter of a Scottish gardener who lived in the Castle Park Road with a large family. She herself had been born in County Meath in 1894. And had worked in this butchers' shop since the age of sixteen. And indeed she was to work there all her life. It was McConaghy's when she started, and she was the bookeeper. She actually lived in the Castle Street butcher's shop stroke house with Charles McConaghy and his wife Sarah. Or so the Census tells me. Though of course it doesn't tell me of her pretty and young in her glass box. And growing old and watching other's lives. But then…I know that anyway. It's a knowing that goes with this trade.

Miss Bethune gave me the change. And I suppose her hand touched mine. Another life, like the college mentor back in bogland, how many lives like that just touch together, briefly? One wonders if they're the real connections, more real than those with lovers friends and children? These latter mere distractions?

One wonders, and moves on.

I left the shop and headed off back home, careful of that change. But not careful enough, I discovered. The ten shilling note that had been the essential part of the change, the very nexus of the change, and that was missing.

I figured out that I must have dropped it. That I hadn't poked it deep enough into the trousers pocket and the cycling had dislodged it in some way. It was a tricky enough moment. My mother was out but when she got back…it didn't bear thinking about. So I applied all the analytical ability available to address the problem. And I figured that maybe I dropped it at the top of Cunningham Hill when I was getting back on the bike after the walk up. That throwing-leg-over-saddle, that sort of movement. Dislodged the ten shilling note. But not the coins because they had dropped to the bottom of the pocket. It was all quite simple and logical. All I had to do was…

Retrace my route.

So I cycled back to Dalkey. On the wrong side of the road, keeping an eye out. And there at the top of Cunningham Hill where the remounting had taken place I got off the bike and mooched carefully around. Sure enough there was the note, in a puddle at the side of the road. Precisely and exactly where I had remounted the bike. Congratulating myself on my intuition I stuffed the note (deep) into my pocket, cycled back home and left the change on the kitchen table. My mother would be none the wiser.

Cathy was very interested in this story. Or, rather, in one particular element of the story. Location location location.

"At the top of Cunningham Hill?" she asked.

"Well just around the coner. There at the bottom of that housing estate."

"Outside Darwin?"

"What's Darwin?"

"A house there on the corner, the Mackens' old house."

"I didn't take the name of the house."

"Darwin" she said. And looked at me. As if to decide. And then decided. "Two men were shot dead in that house," she told me. Matter of factly.

"What's that got to do with the ten shilling note?" I asked.

"No doubt more than we think," she said, and tapped her nose. "There's many things impossible to explain."

"Why were the two men shot dead?"

"Oh I can't tell you that," she said, "you're far too young."

She was obviously prepared to tell me, but needed us to run through the script. I ran through the script.

"Ah go on tell me, I'm fourteen. Nearly fifteen."

"Do you have a girlfriend?"

"Yes Mary, Mary Finnegan, she lives in Silchester Park."

"Is she pretty?"

"Yes very very pretty."

"Well if she left you for another boy, what would you do?"

"I'd beat him up."

"Exactly," said my great aunt Cathy. "Exactly. Egg zackly. And if you were a grown man, if you were a grown man who was also a soldier and had a gun you'd probably shoot him."

"Well I don't know if I'd go that far. Mary Finnegan's not that pretty." I added. But I was just being clever. Because she was. And still is. At sixty something the prettiest journalist in Dublin. Not that the competition is overwhelming.

"It's actually nothing to do with prettiness, it's to do with pride. Man's pride. You'd just have to shoot your rival. It's human nature. And anyway that's what happened. There was a love triangle in that house. Two men were shot dead."

"Why two?"

"One was caught in the crossfire, he had nothing at all to do with the incident. He was in Ireland on holiday. It was just after the war. He'd been a prisoner of war in Germany. Survived that. Got shot in Dalkey."

"That was bad luck."

"None of this has anything to do with luck, young man.."

"Oh. I see." I didn't. "Was he hanged," I asked, " the man who shot them?"

"No, he was mad. Well he wasn't really mad. But he had clever lawyers. And he was locked up in the mental."

"The mental?"

"Madhouse. In Dundrum."

24

"What's his name?"

"I can't tell you, he was a friend of your mother. Ask her."

"I will. Is he still in the mental?"

"No he got out after ten years. Changed his name and went to New Zealand."

"So he got sane?"

"Well no, because he was never mad, just had good lawyers. Very useful to have good lawyers."

"What did he change his name to?"

"I can't tell you that either."

"Well why are you telling me any of it then?"

"Because you're like that tree."

"Tree? What tree?"

"Do they teach you nothing in school? That tree. There's a famous story. A person knows a secret. But can't tell anyone because it's so secret. But has to tell someone. So tells it to a tree."

"Sounds mad."

"Most things do. Anyway the person tells the secret to the tree. Then the tree is cut down and made into a violin. And the violin plays the secret as a tune. And so everyone knows. Surely you know that story?"

"No I don't."

"Well you do now."

I said my goodbye and cycled home. I thought of being a tree. And in the future of being a violin. Turning secrets into tunes. And I reckon now that Cathy got it right, that's more or less the writer's trade. How tuneful are those the tunes…another story. I cycled up Northumberland Avenue, down Corrig Road, and along the Metals. It was dark. I thought of secrets and tunes, and could almost hear them playing in the darkness. And when I was done with those mystical thoughts I brooded on the dead and beautiful twin. Cathy's twin who had died about my age. Young. But not that young that she wouldn't have had breasts. I thought of them, the dead twin's breasts as I pushed the bike up Killiney Hill. And I was still thinking about her and her breasts when I got home.

My mind frequently turned to girls' breasts at that time of night. But not normally dead ones in the ground, maggotty.

"How was Cathy?" my mother asked.

"Well," I said, "the same as ever really."

"So still as mad as a hatter then" said my father.

"She's eccentric," said my mother.

"There's a lot of that," my father noted, and paused. That pause where listeners wait for words. "A lot," he nodded, "in the Conan family."

"She's not actually a Conan," my mother contradicted, "she's a McGovern."

"But they flock together, don't they? Peculiar families. Birds of a feather."

I listened to my parents. Plates and hard heavy objects could fly in that household, but always from my mother's position in my father's direction, never the opposite. Us kids should've been issued with blue berets by the United Nations.

I listened, and then more or less at the time before the banter degenerated into a row I interrupted. It was an art, the timing of that interruption.

"Cathy told me about her twin," I said.

"What twin?" my mother said.

"Her twin, who died, young. At my age. She was beautiful."

"Cathy didn't have a twin," said my mother. And my father snorted. A vindicated sort of snort.

"But she told me…"

"I don't mind what she told you…she didn't have a twin."

"Oh," I said, and left the matter there. And then, still in need of conversation lest my parents had another go at each other, I mentioned that Cathy had also told me about a house in Dalkey where two men were shot dead, a house in Cunningham Road. (I didn't mention the ten shilling note). My parents looked at each other and then my father looked back to his newspaper. *The Evening Mail.* He got it every night. Mandrake the Magician. Heggalamail. All defunct now. Not that my

26

father needs newspapers anymore. He's forgotten news himself.

"Don't be listening to Cathy's stories," said my mother, "filling up your head."

"What was the name of the man who shot the others dead?"

My mother looked at me. "You were hardly born when that happened."

"Cathy said he was a friend of yours."

"We grew up together. Dalkey was a small town then. All the old families knew each other."

"So what was his name?"

"You don't have to know his name. It's all best forgotten. No point in dragging things up. Cathy should know better. Filling up your head. Now go to bed, you're back at school tomorrow."

I went to bed and Cathy died. Not of course on the same night, but not that long afterwards either. I wasn't taken to the funeral but my mother told me in the evening that now I should be glad I used to visit her. Because there was no point in visiting her in Glasnevin. So let that be a lesson.

Point or not, I did visit her in Glasnevin. But it was maybe thirty years later, in my forties. I had become interested in family history. Some people do, at that age. Cathy is buried in an unmarked grave. Unmarked by names, I mean. It is marked in the sense of being properly delineated, laid out with granite kerbs and slabs from Dalkey, loomed over by a huge granite cross. But it is the custom of that side of my family not to mark their names on graves. "Those who know us will know where we are," my great grandfather is reputed to have said. So the McGoverns and the Conans put no names on graves.

May sound crazy to some people...but what did some people ever do for us?

So yes, I did visit her in Glasnevin.

And I also went to Drogheda where she was born. Still on that same family history quest, filling in names and dates, recording. I didn't cycle to Drogheda, doubt if that motorway is conducive to cycling. I drove there and went down the quays and found the house of Captain Michael

McGovern. And yes, there is a plaque on the wall there, a plaque with his name. The name of my great great grandfather. I nodded at the plaque, wondering what new thing now I knew. Not much, I fear. And after that I went to St Peter's Church and met a woman I had arranged to meet, to look at the records. And in the records I found that yes, Cathy McGovern did indeed have a twin. And so she was right and my mother was wrong. Or more likely she was right and my mother just wasn't saying. She must've of course have known about the twin. But she just wasn't saying.

My mother was a secretive woman, and there was a story there. And I wondered what it was. A skeleton best left undisturbed? A tragedy too sorrowful to tell? I didn't know and wanted to ask my mother. But it was far too late to ask her questions then. She was in a nursing home with dementia. And the ghost of my father sat on a bench there across the road, thoughtful. Guarding her.

I drove back to Dublin, and wondered about that twin.

And how beautiful she was.

And her body earth.

And now she rests here on this page, these words her nameless grave.

Caronia

IT CAME UP IN CASUAL CONVERSATION. My mother to my father, or my father to my mother. I'd be sitting there minding my own business…but also keeping an ear to theirs…and I'd hear one or the other of them say it, "the Caronia is in." That phrase seems to have come up almost on a yearly basis, but maybe it wasn't so. Maybe it was such a dramatic event that the memory is enhanced.

That? A dramatic event? We should've gotten out more? Perhaps, but those were quiet times. And the Caronia was a large cuise ship that visited Ireland on its journeys. A large green cruise ship of the Cunard line. Surprising, that green. One didn't expect to see a large green ship anchored out there in the bay off Dún Laoghaire. It was as if it had come from another world, mysterious. And I suppose it did, come from another world. A place of wealth and comfort, of pampering and cocktails at a certain hour.

Cocktails at a certain hour were far from my parents' lives.

Our lavatory paper was torn up squares of newspaper on a string. Not, admittedly, that we were that extraordinarily poor, just that my mother was very very careful. About luxuries. Lavatory paper and jam, those sort of things. Our luxuries then have become today's necessities. Which I reckon is a handy one-sentence-way to define economic progress.

Jam, yes, jam. My mother had a vague rationing system in place concerning jam. It didn't involve coupons, or written records of any sort. It just involved looks. Stern looks as we scooped jam onto our bread.

Followed by an outstretched waiting hand to get the pot safely back to her end of the table. She was economical. And she made her own marmalade in a huge copper preserving pan, a pan inherited from the grand house where she had been born. Do I remember her putting orange pips in a little muslin bag to float in the simmering mixture? Something anyway, there was definitely something in that little bag. (My email awaits news from jam makers). When not in use the preserving pan hung on the scullery wall, shiny. Just as I suppose it once hung in the kitchens of her childhood home. Except back in those affluent days it was the cook would have made the marmalade…while my mother played tennis.

We had no cook. Or television. We actually didn't have much at all. The house was sparse. Yes we did have some grand furniture from the grand houses of yore, sitting there like wealthy relatives at a poorer cousin's wedding…in a kind of embarrassed silence. But generally there was very little. When I was quite young we didn't even have a fridge, or a washing machine. And yes they had been invented. My mother actually had a washboard, though I never saw her use it. (I should have started a skiffle band.) However we did have a car. But that was from and for my father's job. And every year or so it would be replaced. So we did have a new car. And I remember going with him to Brittain's Motors on the Grand Canal to collect a brand new Morris Oxford. The smell of it. I haven't smelled that new car smell since. Writers tend not to. Whatever, the firm, as my father called his employers, the firm wasn't going to have its salesmen going round in any old banger.

They were quite isolated, my parents. Isolated in that Killiney house. No-one ever called. I calculate now that the people they had grown up with had stayed well off, even wealthy, and had drifted away into different social circles. Professional circles. Sometimes the name of a well known surgeon, or solicitor maybe, would come up in conversation somehow, and my father or my mother would say "sure I knew him…when…"

It's an Irish thing that. Though the *when* is usually part of the sentence *when he had no arse in his trousers*. Not so in my parents' case. They knew him when they too were well off kids. But they were separate from all that now and didn't actually seem to have any social circle at all. Yes my father did have one friend, who phoned him up most evenings to have a chat. They rarely met so what they chatted about I have no idea. Work most like, the friend Bob Williams working in the same company. Another travelling salesman. Bob was nephew of a well known artist, Alexander Williams. And the walls of our rooms were hung with his paintings. My sisters inherited them. Though I did manage to wangle one as a gift to my son's wedding. It hangs there now in his house in Rathmines. *A View of Connemara*. And a story of a forgotten friendship.

Granted, there were *some* visitors to my parents' house. Mr Haughton the plumber from the village, he seemed to come a lot. We must've had bad drains. And coal men came. Organised from the Wallace coal office in Dalkey. And I would watch my father counting the empty sacks to ensure he got the full load. And I thought so what's to stop the coalmen bringing in an empty sack with a full, and then leaving both empty on the pile in the garage? Criminal mind of a child? Nah. Lateral. Blue sky thinking. Out of the box, all that.

Other visitors were my grandmother and my aunt, and they would come over from Dalkey on Sunday evenings, and play bridge with my parents. And, very small, I'd watch them, sitting round that large collapsible bridge table, green baize, foldable skinny legs. I'd watch them and listen. And was particularly taken with the concept of dummy. In which one of the four players has to sit there doing nothing whilst the others played. How that dummy was chosen I never quite figured out. And I suppose that's what intrigued. How does one get to be a dummy, watching others play?

Living in this writing game I kind of know the answer now.

Those bridge parties did at least bring a bit of the outside world into the house. Gossip and news. Nothing moved in Dalkey without my grandmother and aunt being on top of the story. Maybe that's where our house first heard *the Caronia has come in*.

Google tells us all...

RMS Caronia was a 34,183 gross register tons passenger ship launched in 1947. She served with Cunard until 1967, and was then laid up in New York until 1974. Sold for scrap, she was being towed to Taiwan when, in a storm, she was wrecked on rocks at Apra Harbour in the Pacific island of Guam.

Yes, a big important ship. To which information I now add, being a small unimportant and insular Irishman, that the modern Irish ferry ship *Ulysses* is 50,938 gross register tons.

One for us!

It would be trite to write, but I have been known to write things trite…why change a winning hand…trite to write that my parents were interested in the *Caronia* because of their own lost wealthy backgrounds. Their world of tennis parties, horses, fun. Their world of cruises even. My mother had lived in Italy in a fair old high style, and my father had been on a cruise just before he was married. Was that some kind of stag event? Not sure. But I do know he went to Madeira. Because on his desk there always stood a little miniature Madeira wine barrel. A souvenir. I rolled it on the floor as a child. And examined it for workmanship as an adult. It was always there, there on the top of his desk which no-one was allowed to open, on pain of! And so no-one did open that desk.. not even himself to my recall! Except sometimes he did move the flap a fraction to stuff in unwanted correspondence, bills and that. And then when he died my sister took it upon herself to open the desk, to catalogue and categorize, and add some glimmer to the family story. But there was nothing in the desk but old bills, telephone, and electricity. And a half empty box of Durex condoms, old fashioned, a something-for-the-weekend-sir sort of packet. Its emptiness a memorial to my unborn siblings.

That's the picture, and whatever the picture paints, bottom line is that my parents were interested in the *Caronia*. For whatever reasons. They were not alone, that interest not at all particular to them. It seems that the great majority of Dún Laoghaire families were very interested indeed in the coming of the *Caronia*. There was always a crowd on the front, rubbernecking. It was a glamorous interlude in a dull time. Nobody had anything much and there was very little happening. True, suburban houses were sprouting huge aerials, scratching the sky for entertainment. But there was little happening up there either. And there were no celebrities. Unless one counted the occasional Irish-American actress in seamed stockings spotted getting off a plane at Shannon. And politicians…oh God…politicians were old men from history books. Men yes, old men, few women of any age in public lfe. Apart of course from actresses in seamed stockings etcetera etcetera.

And so the arrival of the big green ship was an event.

It didn't actually do anything, just sat there in the bay, being green. And why it didn't go into Dublin Port I have no idea. Much larger modern cruise liners seem to access that alright. Maybe Cunard just didn't want to pay the port fees? Who knows. For whatever reason the ship anchored out there in the bay, way out there in fact, and passengers were ferried back and forth to Dún Laoghaire Harbour in little launches. And buses met them there and took them to the scenery of Wicklow, the shops of Dublin.

Tourism generally was in a rudimentary state. Dublin people themselves had only just graduated from going on annual holidays to Bray or Skerries. And incoming visitors still generally made do with Killarney. Jaunting cars. And Great Southern Hotels. Oh but down on Victoria Wharf when the *Caronia* came in…different.

I went down on my bike.

I sat on the bike, leaning against the railing. The spot where the launches came in was just there opposite the *George Yacht Club*. There was a little gated gap in the railing and stone steps leading down to the water. A Cunard functionary stood at this little gate, seeing people up the steps and down the steps. Probably with an eye out for Dún Laoghaire gurriers trying to get a free ride out to the ship. Or indeed, keeping an eye out for me. I did actually try to work out how to penetrate the defences, how to get out to the ship. But soon realised that it wasn't actually possible unless I arrived at the steps on one of those tour buses. Big coffee coloured CIE buses called after the names of Irish rivers. *Slaney. Nore.* And *Lee.* The names painted in flamboyant script over the front windows. *Liffey.*

Tolka. Moy. In winter those buses were stored in the old tram building in Blackrock. I knew these things. A boy on a bicycle does.

No, to get to the ship I'd have to arrive on a bus. And to get on a bus I'd have to start in Glendalough. Or Trinity College, some location where the buses were starting their journey back to the harbour. It all seemed a bit complicated to bother, particularly as I'd be slung off the ship anyway. So I never got to see the *Caronia* close up?

That questionmark is deliberate. Because oh yes I did, I did get to see the Caronia close up. Fifteen years later I was arriving in New York on a ship, another Cunard ship, this one the *QE2*. Myself and my schoolgirl bride stood at the rail, looking at our future. And looking too at the waterfront sights of New York as they were pointed out by the tannoy system.

And on our starboard bow (it said) you will see the *Caronia*. She was a famous Cunard cruise liner. Sad to see her there, moored up, waiting to be scrapped. Some of you Europeans may remember her.

That's what the tannoy said, and yes, at least one of us Europeans did remember her. And he looked out over the rail and yes it was a sad sight. Because she was rusty. And a bit battered looking. And he thought it might have been better not to have seen her like that. To just see her in the memory of when he was a boy on a bicycle.

A boy on a bicycle in Dún Laoghaire, watching the launches shuttling back and forth, and the tour buses arriving back at the quay. From Trinity, and Glendalough, and places like that. And watching the passengers climbing down and streaming towards the steps. Americans mostly, they seemed to me. Middleaged mostly. Their clothes were very different.

And then one particular bus arrived, one which I remember among the many. And another stream of passengers. As they passed I heard one woman say to her companion, "hey that's just another city." Her voice was dismissive. I remember the sound of it clearly, the phrasing, the accent. But can hardly catch a glimpse of the woman herself in memory. Even though I watched, a lot. I watched her walking from the bus, and I watched her going down the steps to the launch, climbing aboard. Those launches had little roofs over maybe two thirds of the hull, and so once aboard I saw her no more. But I did watch the launch itself, chugging off aross the harbour. Watched it until it went out of sight around the end of the East Pier.

Watched it and thought…just another city?

But this is Dublin, my place and my people's place.

How can that be just another city?

The whole thing annoyed me. And I said to myself in an American accent, American language, the American way. (I'd speak it soon enough myself.). "Yeah lady," I said, "and you're just another damn tourist."

And I got on my bike and cycled home.

And now she's dead.

Ghosts

A **WRITER LIVES HIS LIFE** at a permanent crossroads. Good places, crossroads. Known for dancing. And lovemaking. But crossroads are known for ghosts as well, and devils up to devilry. And for the hanging of criminals and awkward citizens. And the burial of vampires, stakes through their hearts. Bottom line…crossroads are for the living and the dying, for getting lost, and for finding one's correct direction. Crossroads are interesting.

Remembering now.

It was an autumnal afternoon and I was reading an interesting old book about the old days around Dún Laoghaire. I was fifteen, thereabouts. And the old book was in my parents' house and it probably came from my mother's family home over in Dalkey. No, there's no probably about it. It definitely came. Defo. Books had not descended from my father's side of the family. Rumours and not-in-front-of-the-children stories yes… but books? No.

The old book mentioned that the crossroads down at the end of Hyde Road was haunted. This to me was interesting. Very. Interesting. Indeed. Particularly on that autumnal afternoon, the windows misty and murky, like they'd been glazed in frosted glass. Windows are eyes to the outer world, and now these were eyes that had gotten cataracts.

And out there the trinity of hills called Dalkey and Killiney and Mullins were mysterious in fog. Oh yes I knew the fog would lift, and the same old hills would re-emerge, the hills I knew from babytime. I knew that. But beneath that knowing there was still a doubt. I just could not be precisely sure. All could've changed. That was the worry. And the ominous boom of the foghorn from Dún Laoghaire Pier did not reassure...things out there could very well be unravelling.

I got out the bike.

"Where are you off to this time of evening?" my father asked. Emphasis on the word *you*. As if there were several boys getting bikes ready, and he was working his way through them.

"I'm going to Dalkey to see David."

I had a friend called David. In Dalkey. I wasn't going to see him. I was going to the crossroads to look for ghosts. But my father didn't do ghosts. He had had something of a difficult childhood. And liked things calm. This calmness extended to avoiding the mystical and the imponderable. And to not being particularly concerned about the activities of teenage boys. So he wandered away with "well it'll be dark soon, make sure you have your bicycle light."

I certainly had. It was of the clip-on variety, battery powered. Exide batteries. Rectangular Exide batteries with strip metal terminals, one long and one short. One either remembers those batteries or one doesn't. Some of my friends had dynamos on their bikes, lighting front and rear. But these were the sort of kids who these days would have iPhones. Or better, the latest thing anyway. Whilst others struggle along, humiliated. In short, a bicycle dynamo was a sophistication beyond my finances. And I needed one, really did. I had mentioned this requirement to my father, but it also seemed to be a sophistication beyond his finances or, more likely, his inclinations. In fact his response to the request for a dynamo was a dissertation on the bicyle lamps in his day. Carbide lamps. I never quite got the carbide lamp. But apparently one poured a mixture of dangerous and corrosive chemicals into the device and in some kind of controlled nuclear explosion the area for a mile or so around was illuminated. Or something along those lines.

I went out the gate and up Killiney Road. Past my friend Sean Collins' house *Orlock* on the left. He changed his name to John and became a lawyer in Sussex. Past my friend John Kingham's house on the right. His older brother David married Helen Hughes. And Helen's younger sister Mary works in Dubray Books in Dún Laoghaire. It all hangs together? In a sort of a way. But onward, boy on a bicycle. Past *Rathale* where the Bardons lived. Mr Bardon was a chemist in Dún Laoghaire. His daughter Jean married Dr Murphy. Past my friend Michael Simmond's house *Fortal* on the left. He founded the *Exchange Bookshop* in Dalkey. Past fat Mr Brownell's house on the left at the corner. *Alberta*, that house. I don't know what he did. He came home (fat) on the 59 bus at regular hours. But keep going, on. Down Dalkey Avenue. Past that house *Seaview* on the left where a respectable family fell on hard times and starved close to death, ashamed to ask for help. Eating cat food, then the cat, that sort of situation. The Veedeepee broke down the door and found them emaciated. Or so my mother said, she knew certain things.

I cycled on. Past the dilapidated cottages where lived the blonde prostitute with beehive hair. She wore a short skirt and teetered on high heels, soliciting in Dún Laoghaire. Hugh Leonard used write about her, but I know not why. All I know is that, just like my mother, I knew certain things. Different certain things than her, but nonetheless. Things are things. The prostitute's mother kept hens. But neither prostitute nor mother nor hens were about as I cycled past. The fog wrapped their cottage in secrets. Like it was cotton wool and there was something precious there to protect. And I suppose there was. But the secrets are gone like the cottages now, fine houses in their place. *Scarsdale* and *St Kitts*.

So cycle on, and ever onwards. Past Mr Morley's nissan hut in the field where he was building *Ard Mhuire Park*. Past the mews where Jimmy lived before he died. *Cul na Binne* they call that site now. Jimmy was a working man, drove a lorry. Everyone knew Jimmy. Backed his lorry into a quarry and was drowned. There was a collection for his widow and children read out at Mass. My mother reached into her handbag. But like she was cleaning a drain, reluctantly. She was a careful woman, needs must. Jimmy had worked building the reservoir in Wilkie's Field. Two other men were killed in a dynamite explosion in that same development. Killed for nothing really, like fallen soldiers in some futile war. Killed for nothing because the reservoir was an engineering failure, and is all demolished now. A flat green field in *Ballinclea Heights*. The playground in one corner is joyless and depressing. And the sculpture is ridiculous. All that field needs is poppies to be Flanders. It has that atmosphere of restless souls…why us?

And does nobody remember?

Perhaps not, nobody but that boy on a bicyle, cycling on down Dalkey Avenue.

Past the small field where an old man grew potatoes. I sometimes talked to him in passing, on my way to visit my granny in Dalkey, or get messages for my mother. I passed this way a lot. But this evening in the fog I wasn't going to visit my granny, or get messages, no, I was heading out in search of ghosts.

A country man, he had accent strange and life unknown. He told me about lazy beds and other things worth knowing in an uncertain world. But his field was empty as I passed in the fog. There's a house called *Marthaven* built there now. It has a huge stone wall as if the future might be dangerous. But it can't keep out the past. Onward, boy on a bicycle in the fog. Past *The Flags* to the right. This pathway led up to an area my mother called *the village*. Dalkey itself she called *the town*. But she went back through generations in the place, and those people had their own language as if they were some sacred caste. And anyway the hillside village was just that, a village. Higgledy piggeldy, planning wise. Clachán-like. Rather like one of the less salubrious districts of Mumbai. A *Slumdog Millionaire* environment. There were tumbledown cottages up there with half doors and hens underfoot in lanes. Pigs in sheds, snuffling. And old women in shawls, watching, always watching. Shawlies, my father called them. They and their cottages were survivors from the quarry days. From squatters and stone men and their women. They made love and thought of God on foggy nights, candlelit. And they and their cottages are gone now, ghosts among words on a writer's page.

But that's the way! So, onwards, down Dalkey Avenue hill. Word of advice. You want to watch your brakes going down there. If your brakes fail you'll hurtle right down into the town and crash through the window of an organic delicatessen. Or a coffee shop. And die amongst bottles of extra virgin olive oil, sacks of Fair Trade beans. Just bear that in mind. Long years ago I bore that in mind, every twenty yards or so of freewheeling testing the bicycle brakes. Just in case. Of course in those days there was no organic delicatessan to crash into. And no such thing as extra virgin olive oil. And fair trade was where you didn't actually shoot your suppliers. But nonetheless, brake failure would have led to the same ultimate conclusion.

Onwards to the crossroads. Yes nowadays there is actually a crossroads at the bottom of Dalkey Avenue, but back in the day it was a T-junction. Not that it mattered, this was not the place that interested me. I had seen no mention of ghosts in this location. But of course I know now that there are ghosts there as well, because one of the Dalkey Castles stood precisely there. It was demolished by the Porter family. They used the stones to build Kent Terrace. (A knowledge of local history is a blessing and a curse). Horace Porter of that ilk kept pigs in a converted tram. And went about Dalkey in a horse and cart collecting food for them. He was a barrister. And my aunt said I don't mind him collecting swill for pigs, but would really prefer he didn't wear a Trinity scarf whilst doing so. That aunt was a punctilious woman. Her name was Aileen but the family called her Polly because of her large parrot-like nose. I also had an uncle nicknamed Bunny because of his buck teeth. Maybe we weren't that sensitive, as a social unit.

I cycled on, down Hyde Road. It was wide and flat and very very foggy. Quite undeveloped then, on either side was mostly fields. Vaguely agricultural, but playing fields among them. Mr Piggott from Albert Road ran a cricket club there. Probably on the playing field of Castle Park School. I played cricket in that club. Wicket keeper. Until the parents of another boy bought him brand new wicket keeping gear. I lost the gig. It was a lesson learned. And anyway it's all built over now. But do those sleeping suburbanites dream the sound of leather striking willow?

Aw forget the cricket. This was ghost hunting time. I cycled on. It was very quiet. I reckon this was because Hyde Road didn't actually lead anywhere, and traffic would go along the parallel tram route. Yes people still called Ulverton Road the tram route in those days, even though the trams were long gone. A desirable house in Dublin generally in those days was described as being *on the tram*. Modern expressions like *on the Dart* and *convenient to the Luas* say much the same thing. Little changes. Wicket keepers apart.

At Hyde Road crossroads I dismounted, and parked my bike against a brambly hedge. But not before turning off the light for the sake of the Exide battery. They cost big money. Well, big money to me. Batteries were available for big money in Mr Coombs' bicycle shop at the end of Castle Street. That building is gone, demolished. It's now a small plaza-like area opposite McCabes (organic delicatessan). On sunny days there's tables there, café society. People with no friends reading *The Irish Times*. Peering over the top of it to catch glimpses of passing celebrities. Bono on his lifts, Maeve Binchy on her walking frame. David McWilliams on his high horse. Modern Dalkey is a sombre tableau, a silent charivari. The destination of aspirational, and a lesson learned. Mr Coombs would be surprised at the social changes. Of course he himself is gone, long gone. He and his brown dustcoat, his bicycle mechanic's oily brown dustcoat, gone. Dust. Ghost.

He had a tandem bicycle, and a wife. And betimes you'd see them cycling along. On Sundays. As a hobby. A day out. Reckon as a couple they were seriously into bicycles. All gone. Him and his mechanic's hands. She and her thrusting thighs, pedalling to his rhythm. (That's a picture best kept veiled.) I remember her as sombre, stoical. And I can hear her ghostly friends mutter how she puts up with a lot with that man. And maybe she did, because I think he was a little mad. But no matter, no matter their moods nor natures, they are ghosts.

I hung around Hyde Road crossroads in the fog. Nothing to see. I wandered around Hyde Road crossroads in the fog. Nothing. I walked up Castlepark Road a little ways, and back again. I walked up Elton Park a little ways, and back again. And then I walked down Castlepark to Breffni Road, the old tram route. And there I watched the cars go by, their headlights making the fog foggier. Then I walked back up to the crossroads. But I stopped outside number two, remembering my mother pointing it out as the home of Elizabeth Clinton, her great great great aunt. Add another great for me. Her father was a butcher. Left a lot of money. Elizabeth inherited and died in 1894, and is buried in Drogheda in the Chord Cemetery. As an adult I went to visit her there but it was locked and chained, against vandals and genealogists alike. I stood there thinking of Elizabeth Clinton for awhile, wondering what she was like. Just as when a boy on a bicycle I had stood outside number two Castlepark Road wondering what she was like. I knew she was an artist because my mother had some of her drawings. But about her, what was she like? As a boy I decided that she had big breasts, being an artist...like. And though there was a logic to that decision at the time it completely escapes me now.

I walked back to the crossroads.

I took the bike out of the brambly hedge. I turned on my bicycle lamp. Old fashioned even in those days, it turned on with a little screw down device to close the terminals. It gave a pathetic light. But then the point of bicycle lamps is to let other road users see you, not the other way round. I got up on the bike and sat there, one foot on the ground, the other on a pedal.

Disappointed, I had seen no ghosts.

I cycled home.

And yes I know now that the Hyde Road Crossroads is on the ancient route between Bulloch and Monkstown castles. And there may well be ghosts there, and maybe I was just unlucky. Maybe there are lots of ghosts there. And even if not, there surely has to be one. One ghost, making his or her way endlessly between the castles. Perhaps with a cart of fish?

His or her?

A girl ghost, I do feel it is a girl ghost. Definitely now, yes it's all becoming clearer, the fog is lifting. It's a girl ghost with artists' breasts like my great great great aunt Elizabeth Clinton. Yes yes, the fog is clearing, and it's all firming up. I note that those ghostly breasts are almost identical to Molly Malone's at the bottom of Grafton Street. Except Molly's are bronze and the ghost's are dreams. But nonetheless, nonetheless the girl ghost I see is actually dressed very much like Molly Malone at the bottom of Grafton Street. Although her feet are bare, and her hair tangled. Because she is poor in poorer times. And every day she travels between Bulloch and Monkstown castles. Her fishcart swaying, her thoughts wandering. Every day. Alone. But she is not lonely.

How could she be lonely? That book from my mother's house was right. There are indeed many ghosts in the vicinity of Hyde Park crossroads. It's coming down with them. Lookit. There goes Mr Coombs on his tandem with the wife behind. And there's that blonde prostitute I knew once. She teeters on high heels, a child playing grownups. And there's the fat man who lived at the top of Killiney Road. And that respectable couple, who starved because they were proud. And curly haired Jimmy, he died in a quarry. And an old country man who knew about potatoes, and how to grow them. And shawlies leaning over half doors, their grandchildren would sell the sites for big money. But nothing would change. And things would go on, every birth buying death.

We are surrounded by ghosts. Different ghosts for different days. And today's ghost is a boy on a bicycle, himself searching for ghosts. And not knowing that he had found them. That they were all around him. And if they weren't ghosts yet, they soon would be.

As he himself would be.

And all he knew.

Pigeons

HE DIDN'T RECOGNISE ME. But then why should he? It was thirty years ago, and he was almost the same number of years older than me. And that makes a total of fifty years between us. And of course there's the thing where younger pupils in a school know the older, not the other way around. Not that we were pupils in a school. And even if we'd been the same age at the same time we wouldn't have gone to the same school. No way. I went to school in St Conleth's in Ballsbridge and he worked for the Corpo in Dún Laoghaire. You don't have to do the math on that one. There is a mutual exclusivity there. St Conleth's has surely produced its share of drunks, criminals and wife beaters…but Corpo manual labourers?

Digging holes in roads?

That's where I saw him first, passing on my bicycle. Digging holes in roads. There were far less mini-diggers in those days, more muscle power. Men personally dug holes in roads, pick and shovel. I knew all about them, their customs and routines. Like how when they packed up for the day they put a little barrier around the hole and went home. Then at evenfall another man arrived. And he put boxy paraffin lamps around the barriers to the hole, warning lights. Then he went into the little hut provided, the night watchman's hut. And he sat there and for warmth there was a brazier in front of the hut. Fired by Alco, a type of coke. And around the back of the hut there'd be a pile of this Alco stuff so that every so often the watchman could replenish his fire. Sometimes he cooked sausages. And almost always he was drinking tea, contemplating.

I saw all this, learned all this cycling round the borough in the dark. On nocturnal jouneys barely remembered as to purpose or direction. No doubt it was because I went to school in the city that my friends were scattered far and wide. And commuting around the suburbs was necessary for social interaction. Bicycle commuting. So that got me out at night and also in the day...those journeys also mysterious as to purpose or direction...quite similar to the night, just the daylight version. And in that daylight I would see him, digging holes.

The man whom I recognised as a hole digger, the man who didn't recognise me, back then he stood out among the rest. Just...stood out. Admittedly not that far because he was usually waist deep in a hole. In any event he wasn't that big, but what there was of him was obviously strong. Shovelfuls of earth would come up from the hole like there was a cartoon gravedigger down there. And so all in all I knew him well... from the waist up, that being the part I'd see protruding from the hole. Well built, he rippled. But with only enough muscle to do the job in hand. No surplus for display or statement. On sunny days he'd be stripped to the waist. But there are not that many sunny days in Dún Laoghaire, and usually he was dressed. Never against the rain though. Jesus those were tough times. Men in outdoor manual jobs in those days didn't seem to wear any sort of uniform or protective gear. Not sure if they even do much now, apart from hi-vis jackets. But back then anyway people's work clothes were just the same as any other time. Just shabbier, looking like worn out versions of their Sunday gear, of their nights out in the pub. I remember all that. And my memory classification system sardonically notes that I mostly remember this particular road worker on sunny days.

He was not precisely like a Greek God, but heading that way. If I had been older and gayer and more versed in Classical mythology I'd certainly have promoted him to that position. But I wasn't. I just thought he was a pretty damn strong guy, down there digging that hole. Now that I am more versed in Classical mythology I'll grant him the Greek God thing. And not only for the understated just-right-physique but because, in addition to all that he had the curly hair which carves so well in marble. He didn't wear it in a lacquered quiff, slathered with Brylcreem, as was the fashion then, but just left it there curly on the forehead. As was the fashion in ancient Greece. Presumably. According to statues anyway. But did ancient Greeks actually have that curly hair? I don't know much about Greeks...ancient or indeed modern...but I do have a suspicious analytical mind. And I wonder, chicken 'n egg sort of wondering: did those gay-as-pink-ink sculptors come first, picking out curls with their little chisels? And then did the actual hairstyles come next? Life imitating art?

We'll never know.

I met him first just there at the back of the East Pier, around where there's an antique cannon now. But it wasn't there then. I remember it somewhere else, but not precisely where that somewhere was. No doubt my email will inform me when this book flies off the shelves. The People's Park? Perhaps. Haigh Terrace? Could be.

He was feeding the pigeons. Their descendants still gather there. I stood astride the bike and watched. And we got into conversation. He knew an awful lot about pigeons. And pointed out the different markings of the different types. Up to then I had thought pigeons all the same. Grey. With a strange ability to annoy. Up to then I didn't really know that pigeons came in different types, different habits, different breeding. But up to then I reckon I didn't know either that much the same applies to people.

"They homing pigeons?" I asked.

"No, feral lads mostly. Some of them though. Homing pigeons who haven't gone home."

He laughed, as if he thought that might be a very good idea. Laughed and scattered grain. And those pigeons weren't his only thing. He pointed out a cormorant on the rocks below. And told me about cormorants. And he told me it was kind of his hobby, walking down the pier, looking at the birds. And I being a smartass boy on a bicycle I responded with "why bother, the same ones are walking here." And I nodded towards a girl passing. To point her out, man to man. Or, rather, boy on a bicycle to man. His nose wrinkled and he snorted. And said "no not those sorts of birds, who'd be interested in them?"

Well me for starters, I thought, I would. And watched the girl go by..

"Don't be bothering with her," he said, "she's just trying to get you going, wiggling her fat arse like that."

"She's just walking, girls walk like that."

"Yeah because they've got fat arses, to get you going. My advice... don't fall for it."

I shrugged, OK. The sort of shrug that comes in response to advice that may not be entirely appropriate to one's own situation.

"Do you want to come down the pier, look at the birds," he said. "The feathery ones," he added, with a grin.. "Lots of different ones at the back of the pier. You wouldn't believe. Very very interesting."

"Oh God I'm meeting people in the baths," I said. And pointed at my togs on the carrier as if I had to prove that I was, that I wasn't just making excuses.

"Oh well another time so," he shrugged. "I'm here most Thursdays."

"Why Thursdays?"

"Payday."

"The pier is free."

"We get off early on Thursdays. Most fellows go to the pub. I come down here. Healthier. Go to the pub later of course. But never like pubs in daylight. My father was like that too."

"Was he?"

"Yes," he said, "he was."

And that was about it. I cycled off.

Beside Dún Laoghaire baths there was and still is a small railed off enclosure, and this was the bicycle park. The railings on one side are designed in such a way as to take the front wheel of a bike, an early edition of those modern street furniture yokes one sees trendily dotted around the cityscape. Not that the modern ones are primarily there for the convenience of cyclists, no, they are there merely to imply that your city fathers and mothers are right up there to the environmental minute.

I parked and locked the bike. To the railings of course. That bike was my lifeline. I took my togs. Swimming togs in those days were carried in a sort of swiss roll made from a towel. There were tightly wrapped swiss rolls and sloppy ones. It all depended on the personality of the swimmer. I removed my (medium tight) swiss roll from the back carrier. Yes, back carrier, and I'm not ashamed. This was a workaday bike. There was no nonsense about the machine. It had many functions to perform. The swimming gear removed from the carrier, I turned around. And there they were, chatting.

Mr Gillespie and Mr McGovern.

Mr Gillespie was wearing a boater hat. But then he was always wearing a boater hat. So much so that in memory now the hat wears him. No doubt this is because Mr Gillespie himself is but vaguely drawn in the mind, and I just have to remember the hat. His features are a mystery. All I can do now is to recollect him as the sort of man who would in fact wear a boater hat, and moreover wear a boater hat in the Dún Laoghaire of 1960, thereabouts. That took some wearing.

Not young, I remember that, and in fact so not young that he was probably born in the place called Kingstown. A gentleman, another detail, in accent and demeanour, he may very well have been a Protestant. But I do wonder now...is Gillespie a protestant name? Gillespie... MacGiolla Easpaigh? Son of the bishop's servant? Ah sure who can tell at this remove?

Mr Gillespie was the swimming teacher in the baths. He had actually taught me myself to swim. And I remember his interesting methods. (However, none of these involved, as with the case of modern swimming teachers, sexual abuse.) His methods were simple, straightforward. The central plank of his system was to tie a flotation device around the child, tie a rope to that device, and then tell the child to wade out into the pool as far as the rope allowed. Interestingly, no matter how tall or small the child, that rope always just stretched far enough to get the child to the point of panic and half drowning. A type of early waterboarding, I reckon. The pupil was then told to turn around and face the teacher. Whereupon Mr Gillespie would tow the child back to the edge of the pool by the rope. The bank, I believe the term for the edge of the pool in swimming circles. So there we have it. Mr Gillespie pulling the rope, the child thrashing around wildly, sinking, almost drowning, but getting there eventually. The story of life itself. It worked for me. I became a good swimmer. If a good swimmer with a marginal interest in bondage.

So there I was, in the bike park of the baths, and there was this Mr Gillespie, talking to this Mr McGovern. They were men of a certain age, and perhaps not the marrying kind. Even if they were married. And perhaps they were a couple of old queens, in modern parlance. I have no idea. Well I do actually, but judge not lest we be, and first stone, cast, and all that.

Mr McGovern was wearing a bowler hat. Or a hat that was definitely somewhere along the lines of being a bowler. Approaching bowlerdom. He always wore that hat. It wasn't strictly bowler, not London city gent, but it certainly did have strong bowler tendencies. And that is about all I can remember about that hat. But, the mind compensates. Because, in the case of Mr McGovern, quite in contrast to that of Mr Gillespie, I can remember the actual man quite well.

And why wouldn't I? Mr McGovern was my great-uncle, whereas Mr Gillespie was simply my swimming teacher. He worked as a commercial traveller for Todd Burns, a department store and wholesale drapery business based in Dublin's Mary Street. He was, in short, a man who was positively Joycean, a Mr Bloom. Dublin was actually full of them in Edwardian times, and it's never quite clear (to me) why Joyce is extolled for capturing their essence. They were hanging out of the lampposts.

The Todd Burns building is now a Penneys. And Mr McGovern's father, Michael McGovern, had been general manager of the store. Michael was my great grandfather. So the bowler hatted Mr McGovern was family. And he comes to the page equipped with family facts and anecdotes.

His signature announced himself as *Robert*, but he was *Bob* to the world at large. A canny enough man, his hobby was stocks and shares, a hobby which paid off. Well, at least it paid off for one of my sisters, his godchild, and for my mother too. My own godmother was a Royalette, a theatrical dancer. She left me nothing but her sense of fun and humour. Whereas Bob, he left his goddaughter my sister and my mother his niece a fair old wodge of money. Not to mention his house up the town. And why wouldn't he? He lived a modest life. And played bridge. I know that, and I also know that he was partial to a *Russian Steam Bath* because I frequently saw him about the baths. And knew that he went into the innards, which was a cavern of hissing steam and shiny copper pipes. And cubicles mysterious.

Now I personally haven't a notion what a Russian steam bath is. I never went that far into that cavern. But I suspect it may be a type of box one sits into, with one's head sticking out a hole in the lid. Like a malefactor waiting for rotten fruit to be thrown, that sort of situation. Yes of course I could google *Russian Steam Bath*, but I prefer there to be a certain mystery about certain things. In the same way I could google what-do-lesbians-actually-do…but I like that to be a mystery too.

Mr Gillespie and Mr McGovern…I talked to these two misters for a while. Grown up a bit from when I had dealings with them last, I suppose I was a stranger to them now. Neither of them were too hot on the social intercourse thing so the conversation was short. Three people scratching around for words to put together. So it was brief encounter. And anyway I had to go in to meet my mates and do the lengths. Yes I was doing lengths. The Olympics were round the corner.

I did my lengths and swimming up and down I thought of them, those three men. The three men of my last half hour. All so different and all so much the same. The Pigeon Man. And Mr Gillespie. And Mr McGovern. I thought of them and wondered, what is the pattern, and how precisely do three disparate people one meets on the same afternoon fit together? And what is the story there, what the connections? But conclusions came there none. I suppose they don't, not to a teenage boy swimming up and down a swimming pool. Not to a teenage boy drying and changing, and guys flicking wet towels at your arse. That hurt. Judged well, if the flick occurred precisely as the towel landed on the buttock, that really hurt. And you'd be conscious of your backside for some considerable time after. Conscious of the pain for a while and then, when that faded, just conscious of your flesh. And it bothering you.

After my swim and changed again I cycled back home to Killiney, this time taking the unofficial People's Park route. No doubt then as now this in contravention of several Bye Laws and regulations. But cyclists then as now were unconcerned with piffling regulations. We are free spirits. Can't take that away from us. Life may be bitter and harsh and unjust, but the only thing that it can really take away from us is life itself. As Mr Gillespie and Mr McGovern now know well. Or know not at all, as the case may be. And as for the pigeon loving working man, he too, he's probably also dead. Though I did see him in recent times. Well, if recent times be maybe twenty years before I write these words.

He didn't recognise me. But then why should he? It was thirty years ago, and he was almost the same number of years older than me. And that makes a total of fifty years between us. I saw him in Dún Laoghaire Post Office in the queue. A long queue, most of the post office clerks doing those mysterious things behind *sorry dúnta* signs, mysterious things which preclude any dealings with the customers.

In front of me there was a group of elderly men, their faces vaguely familiar. There are several types of that vagueness. And this was the one applied to faces that one had known when they were young, faces now grown old. Those sorts of faces. I recognised them. They were DúnLaoghaire Corporation manual workers. Street sweepers, bin men, diggers of holes. And I worked it all out. And realised that they were here together because this was a Thursday, and they were all holding cheques which they were waiting to cash. Pension pay cheques, I reckoned they collected them in the Town Hall every week that particular day. And this was a regular little gathering of old comrades, a social event. And I supposed some of them went for a few pints after. And remembered their dead in the way of old men. As if talking of the dead will keep they themselves alive.

So I thought all this.

And there among the group was the man who loved the pigeons. And I looked at him there in the post office, remembering. He was an old man now but I remembered him different.

And then the queue moved on.

Mollie and Tess

MOLLIE HAD A LAWNMOWER made in hell. Some hellish workshop specifically organised to turn out troublesome machines...as punishment for the many sins of teenage boys. Her lawnmower was of complex and inefficient design, a uselessness compounded by the rust of years. A push machine, its default mode was to bury its head in the ground like an ostrich. It did not glide, it jammed and gouged. And was a right pain in the neck.

My job to cut her grass with this.

Weekly in the summer I cycled over.

Did the job and weakly cycled back.

Mollie lived in a house called *The Octagon* on Ardeevin Road in Dalkey. She was my Grandmother and her neighbour was Johnny Wadham the drummer. I never looked forward to cutting her grass, but I did look forward to meeting Mollie. So I'd go, not that I'd any choice in the matter. My mother was on the case.

I'd cycle up Killiney Road, and down Dalkey Avenue, along Cunningham Road and down to Ardeevin. Mollie's house was right opposite the pedestrian railway bridge. Or, rather, the entrance to her house was opposite the bridge. Quirky enough, it led to a long pedestrian pathway up a hill through trees. There was no vehicular access. And I often wondered and maybe still do wonder how Mollie got her Bechstein grand piano up to the house. One of life's mysteries.

I'd hide my bike behind the tree at the bottom. Behind the trunk of the tree, these being serious trees. Beech, I know now, with their silvery trunks. And sycamores with aeroplanes of seeds. Leaving the bike there I'd walk up that long pathway to her house. And my walk would frequently be accompanied by the sound of drumming from next door. Johnny Wadham, a professional musician, at practice. I would imagine myself to be someone living in the days of Empire. Living, but about to die. Because I was heading for execution to the sound of warning drums. On a parade ground in India. That girl in the sari watching…I will die with our secret…all that…

"The grass is too wet to cut today," Mollie told me. "we'll go down the town instead."

"Down the town?"

"I plan to do a big shop in Findlater's, you can carry the bags back."

"A big shop?"

"Sugar. And butter."

"How big is that?"

"Sugar weighs a pound. Butter too. I may get four pounds of each, to keep me going."

"Should do the trick."

"Though the butter might go off. So maybe I'll get six pounds of sugar and two pounds of butter. It'll be the same weight."

"Eight pounds. Why don't you get a fridge?"

My mother had recently got a fridge. A big fat curvy American-looking refrigerator. It sat in the kitchen like a Cadillac parked in a farmyard.

"I have a larder, " she protested, offended. And so she did. A larder with a wire screen door to keep out the flies and let in cool air.

"It's not the same as a fridge though," I told her.

"A larder was good enough for your grandfather."

"There were no fridges back then. They're a modern invention."

"Oh well he would have had one so. He was a very modern man. Had the first telephone in Dublin."

"Who did he phone up?"

"Everyone asks that."

We went down the avenue.

"That bike of yours will be stolen," Mollie said, pausing by the last tree. "They'd take the eye out of your head."

"It's locked."

"You don't think that'd stop them. Steal it, lock and all. Take the eye out of your head. That's why I wear my jewellery going out. Burglars."

"My bike has never been stolen before."

"Only takes the once."

We walked on.

A roadsweeper was scuffing at the pavement opposite the gate. Scuffing at weeds with a spade. I noticed how the blade of the spade was worn to a sharpness and a curve. And thought of the years of its work.

"Good afternoon, Mrs Conan" he said.

"Good afternoon, Mr Murphy" she responded. "That's a fine day."

"So long as it keeps dry" he said.

"Oh I think it will" said Mollie with glance to the sky. "The rain is gone. For now."

"It was really something."

"It was."

She reached into her handbag, took out her purse, removed a coin and handed it to him. "Something for the children" she said.

"Thank you Mrs Conan" said Mr Murphy. And made a vague as-if-to-touch-a-cap gesture. He wasn't wearing a cap. But the gesture was probably somewhere in his dna.

We walked on across the railway bridge.

"He'll spend that on beer," I said, "not his children."

"Yes but the fact that he spends that on beer will mean there'll be more money available for the children."

"No, he'll just buy more beer."

"You're a very cynical young man. Try to think the better of people."

"I will."

"I always give him a half crown when he's around."

"That's quite a lot of money."

"I have quite a lot of money. Though sometimes I don't have an actual half crown coin. So I give him a two shillings instead."

"You could add a sixpence."

"I could, but that might be pretentious, and calculating. One should not be calculating in one's charity. Your grandfather started the Vincent de Paul in Dalkey, did you know that?"

"Yes, you told me."

"He was a very charitable man you know. Was chairman of Dalkey Town Commissioners."

"I know, you told me that too."

"Pity you never knew him."

"If you keep telling me things about him I'll know him well enough."

"But it's not the same. You're only knowing him second hand. Like reading a book. He's a character in a book. To you. Do you read Dickens?"

"Not really."

"You should, lots of characters in Dickens. I have a set of all his works."

"I know, I've seen them."

"I may leave them to you in my will. But don't count your chickens. I may not."

"I'll wait and see what happens."

"That'd be best. Old ladies can be fickle."

"And young ladies?"

"Fickler," she said, and laughed. And her laughter was the sound of that photo on the Bechstein grand piano. That silver framed photo of Mollie as a young woman. She had been quite beautiful. But was she fickle? How could I know? Though I did know that my father said she hadn't talked to her husband for the ten years before he died. He was an older man. She was a second wife. It happens.

We walked down Railway Road.

"Do you know," she said, "I met a woman in the town the other day and she said hello Mrs Conan you're looking very clean. Imagine saying that. Clean. What did she mean?"

"Perhaps that you were wearing bright clothes?"

"Do people want me to wear black? Am I Queen Victoria?"

"She was giving you a compliment."

"I'm none too sure about that, none too sure. She comes from Tubbermore Avenue."

"What's that got to do with it?"

"I've never met an honest person from Tubbermore Avenue. Except Miss Humphries the dressmaker."

"You can't write off a whole road like that."

"I'm not writing off a whole road. Miss Humphries is an honest woman. And the Homans. They'd be honest. But they're Protestants so it doesn't count."

"I don't follow."

"Protestants are honest anyway. It's no virtue to them, just natural."

We went into Findlater's shop. It had counters. With people my father called counter jumpers behind them. Some in brown dust coats, others in white, dependant on the speciality of the particular counter. The man at the sugar counter was wearing a brown coat. His colleague at the butter wore white. It was that sort of shop. There were barstool-like stools every so often along the counters and my grandmother perched on one while the brown coated man filled sugar bags. He hoped she was keeping well.

"Excellent, thank you," she said.

We then moved on to the butter, and my grandmother perched on a stool while the man in a white coat cut and patted chunks of butter into pound weight shapes. He hoped my grandmother was keeping well.

"Excellent, thank you," she said.

Thus we moved about the counters. And over our heads whizzed little canisters on wires, bringing cash from the counterjumpers to the cashdesk, and change from the cashdesk back to the counterjumpers. An aerial system, something Alpine about it. Or so I thought back then.

The cashier was a woman, although heavily moustached.

I wondered at that, but I suppose a boy does.

All part of life in Dalkey Town for a boy on a bicycle. But of course those times ended, and I grew up and moved away. And it was many years before I came back to the area to live in the town.

My wife H and I came back from somewhere far and foreign and she bought a house in Dalkey. It fell to H to buy the house because I was not currently in the appropriate financial situation to so do. *Broke* is the technical term. My grandmother Mollie was long dead by then, and probably just as well. She died while I was away. And my mother wrote and told me she'd left me a set of Dickens. And did I want it sent to Africa?

I said no, hang on to them, I'll read them when I get back.

Things were bad enough in Africa without *Little Dorrit* by my bed.

Bottom line...my grandmother would have been horrified to see a grandson living in White's Villas. Explaining to her that we were, if not part of a wave, at least part of the first trickle of gentrification would have been pointless. To my grandmother the likes of serving maids and gardeners and that class of citizen lived in Whites Villas. Not to mention road sweeping men like Peter Murphy.

Yes, he who had once had been the roadsweeper lived a few doors down. But no longer a humble roadsweeper, now the jovial caretaker of Dalkey Town Hall, we shared a scoop or two in *The Queen's* betimes. And discussed Dalkey matters. Of people and times that blow-ins like Bono and Pat Kenny would not know. And he remembered Mrs Conan of Ardeevin Road. A decent woman. And I remembered way back and knew just why he thought that, because she gave him half a crowns.

And then one day one of his young daughters came to my door, and said you make books, don't you? And I told her yes, that I worked in publishing. And she told me enthusiastically that she drew, and painted, and how could she get her drawings and paintings into books, she'd like that. I told her to bring the drawings round, and I'd see what advice I could give. But she never did. Then a few months later I picked her up at the busstop in Dún Laoghaire, and gave her a lift to Dalkey. She was bubbly, early twenties, and attractive. And wore a very short skirt, an invite to the eyes, *RSVP... respondez s'il vous plait. J'ai responde...*and I looked at her knees and her thighs beside me in the car. And thought thoughts. Men do. Get used to it. The fleshier the area of the thigh, the paler the darkness of the tights, that sort of observation. And I particularly noted the almost white of her knees coming through the dark of the tights. The way the fabric stretches there. I don't know why I noticed that. My background in design, I suppose. That, or lust.

Off we went. Along George's Street. Past the People's Park. Summerhill and the Glasthule Road. Through Glasthule itself then Sandycove. Past *Fitzgerald's Pub*. And there I vaguely thought I'll ask her in for a drink. But quickly decided that to be completely inappropriate. Seeing as she lived only three doors away from me. If she had lived a few streets away it might have been a different question. The appropriateness of dalliance with a young woman is in inverse proportion to the distance between her residence and that of one's wife. So I just drove on. Past that grim redbrick house where my great grand aunt Mary Carroll once had lived. She had the fear of being buried alive, common in her times. So by instructions willed they slit her wrists before they buried her. Or so Mollie had told me in one of our conversations.

"Why? I asked.

"Blood doesn't flow from a corpse," was Mollie's answer.

Mary Carroll had inherited that house from her own aunt, my great great grand aunt Elizabeth Clinton. Elizabeth the artist. Elizabeth the sombre artist, the sombre heavy breasted artist who had inherited big money from her father William Clinton, a wholesale butcher in Drogheda. She never married. A pity really.

I noted all this in my head as I passed. Like a computer my brain has the ability to do several things simultaneously. It's all about the RAM, or maybe ROM. Whatever. In this instance anyway it enabled me to drive the car, to admire the thighs of my companion, and to recollect small anecdotes and historical details of locations passed.

It's a gift I suppose.

Drove on. Past *Bulloch Castle* and *The Manor*. And thought of the old in there, waiting for visitors and death. And how the first was doubtful, the second certain. And I thought fuck that, that future, that death. Fuck death. Maybe I should put a hand on this girl's leg, there seems to be a chemistry. But then somewhere there at the start of Ulverton Road I got sidetracked. And remembered, and mentioned her drawings, and told her that she'd never come around with them. And she said she must. But she'd gotten into music, big time. Writing songs and that. But one day she'd bring around the drawings. One day. But she never did. And she went away, and out of touch.

The shit hit the fan in White's Villas not long after.

Her brother hanged himself in the Murphy house. And another brother vanished, his body never found for years. And older sisters came back from England with stories of incest and abuse. And tales of a newborn baby killed, stabbed with knitting needles. The tabloids went apeshit, and Peter Murphy and his wife were taken in for questioning. And then the police took over the house. And ripped up floorboards and dug the garden. But they found nothing. I don't suppose they were looking for the right thing.

I actually reckon there is no finding, not of answers anyway. But I am kind of sorry that I never saw the daughter's drawings. They might have made the cover of a book. A book that wanted nothing but the writing, the writing of a happy ending. But there wasn't to be any happy ending. She hanged herself in a flat in Cabra.

Her name was Theresa.

I knew her as Tess.

Sleep on… child.

Parents

THEY WERE THE QUINTESSENTIAL Dublin Jewish couple. He a doctor and she blonde, bejewelled. Not quite over the top, but definitely near the summit of personal decoration. They stood apart, they stood out. And other parents made wry remarks… but out of hearing. Being polite, like. I reckon they were the sort of remarks made by German couples in the nineteen twenties, early thirties. Remarks about their Jewish fellow citizens. Nothing vehement or vitriolic, but just enough to separate, to classify. And just enough to seperate, to classify, well that's usually just about enough…to get the ball rolling. And we all know where that ball rolls.

My mind sees them now at the back of the West Pier in Dún Laoghaire. There was a junior sailing club there, for juniors. Nothing elaborate no, just a fenced-off enclosure with a shipping cotainer acting as combination lock-up and changing room. It wasn't posh or exclusive in any way. Founded by the *Dublin Bay Sailing Club* to introduce young people to sailing, it formed some kind of recruitment drive. But it hardly spread the net that wide, the majority of teenagers there being children of members of one or other of the big Dún Laoghaire yacht clubs. And the minority? Well, people like myself, and people like the son of this Jewish couple, we who had no family connection to the world of Dublin sailing.

I wasn't connected because my parents just weren't the sailing types. Granted my Grandfather had once had a very large yacht, but he lost all his money and left my father poor. Maybe that had something to do with it, yachts and boats were unnecessary fripperies to my parents. The Jewish couple I mention most likely had their own reasons for not being involved in watery things. Fact is, there weren't that many Jewish people in the big Dún Laoghaire yacht clubs in those days. Being Jewish was no great help in the application process. I suppose they could get in, but it was eye of the needle sort of stuff. Those were the days that were in it. A similar situation obtained for Dublin golf clubs, only more so. In fact. so much more so that the Jewish community founded their own golf club. And then later, as land as upon sea, they were instrumental in founding the *Dún Laoghaire Motor Yacht Club.*

The son of the quintessential Dublin Jewish couple was a contemporary of mine in the junior sailing club. He was, well, the quintessential son of a Dublin Jewish couple. Dark, bespectacled and vaguely nerdy, his destiny flapped about him like the wave of a flag. And other times it just stood silently by his shoulder…like one of those advertising placards held by illegal immigrants in Grafton Street promoting tourist traps up alleyways. But no matter, whether flapping or still, his destiny always said *doctor, our son the doctor,* or maybe (at a pinch) *lawyer.*

They always seemed to be there, those Jewish parents. Up on that concrete wall looking down at us as we launched the dinghies. Watching us through binoculars as we sailed out in the bay. Waiting for us as we came back in with tales of win or loss. Well, not waiting for *us,* waiting for their son. I noticed that and thought it…nerdy…perhaps. But I think it different now. Because I also noticed that my own parents rarely if ever appeared on the wall or indeed anywhere in the vicinity of my sailing career. And I to be one of the stars of the junior sailing world!

But then…my parents were what English uppercrust Oxbridge students define as *dry bobs*…as distinct from *wet bobs.* Very sporty yes, but their sports were dry. Took place on solid land. Rugby. Tennis. Golf. Those for my father, my mother substituting hockey for his rugby. She had been a member of the *Maids of The Mountains* hockey club. I remember that because as a teenager I wore a scarf that I found in the attic at home. A *Maids of The Mountains* hockey club scarf. I also found her little tennis skirts up there. Folded and ironed in careful pleats. When did she think she would need them...again? I reckon she didn't realise that much of life has no *again* attached. That things go on. It's a trap folks fall into, thinking like that. But traps snap and there are endings.

So yes, her tennis days were over and I wore her hockey scarf. But her skirts no, the scarf was enough. And yes it'd be nice to be able to report that as a teenager I did wear my mother's little tennis skirts. Secretly, in the attic. Like a character in *Psycho*. And I'd probably sell more books on foot of that news. But I didn't, so I can't. And it's too late now. I no longer have the figure. And back then it was just scarfs I was into, the bronchitis. Not a good condition for a boy who lived on top of a hill, a boy who got around on a bike. Cycling up the steeper parts of Killiney Hill with other boys there was always a kind of macho competition, to see who could get the furthest before giving up and getting off and walking. I always lost. But there again, I frequently had the prettiest girlfriend.

The bronchitis. My mother recommended keeping the chest warm. And keeping her happy was more important than discussing her dodgy medical theories so I wore scarfs. Yes I was really big into scarfs. I also betimes wore the scarf of one of my uncles. He had been in the RAF, and so that was an RAF scarf. Strangely its colours were much the same as those chosen by the maids up the mountains. Where my maids' scarf is gone now I have no idea. But I do still have that RAF scarf. It's folded neatly in a drawer, a drawer I never open. And as I type that sentence I hear the shade of my mother mocking...when did you think you would need it again?

Well, I may wear it at Bodenstown, or Arbour Hill one day.

Bottom line in all this...unlike that Jewish couple, my own parents rarely came to the sailing club to watch me sail. My mother's motherly Jewish blood diluted through the generations? Perhaps. And I suspect... no, more than that, I have evidence...I have definite evidence to confirm that even if they had been wet bobs, even then they would not have shown much interest. That evidence? I also played tennis, a distinctly dry bob activity, in *Glenageary Tennis Club* in Silchester Road. Cycled there on the bike, the racquet across the handlebars. White socks. White shorts. White shoes. White boy in the leafy suburbs. And my parents' shadows never fell upon the courts those sunny afternoons.

I lived my life alone, a boy on a bicycle, cycling up and down from Killiney to Glenageary, or from Killiney to the back of the West Pier in Dún Laoghaire. Well, alone in the orphaned sense, but there were companions. My friend Brian. He died of the heroin. My friend David. He joined the RAF. Whoops...lightbulb flashes in my mind. I could sell him my scarf. Oh but he's probably retired. Or if he's not I don't want to be standing under one of their planes. So we'll forget that, and move on. And move on to the memory of a girl called Dairine. She was Dairine O'Kelly, daughter of Professor Cormac O'Ceallaigh, a physicist in the *Institute of Advanced Studies*. Involved in the evolution of nuclear fission, and thus of the bomb, if he were Iranian today then Mossad would get him. Dairine herself became a Professor in the University of Lille. Author of *La Syntaxe Raisonnée*. De Boeck Université 2003... *Du genre à l'individu dans la détermination du nom (Étude Comparée de l'Anglais, de l'Irlandais et du Français).*

Jesus that Google is great.

For some reason Professor-to-be Dairine always seemed to be on my crossbar hurtling down Killiney Hill. And I cannot think of why. She wasn't actually a girlfriend, and I never seemed to have gone back up the hill with her. Fortunate really, because now as I type her name I remember her as a largish girl. And I did suffer from bronchitis.

I suppose in life there's downhill girls and uphill girls.

Memories of one summer, all this, well maybe two, three at most. Three of those summers just before something else, a war, a death, a love affair. If memory were a book this one would be a dropped cap at the start of a chapter. (A typographical term, so reader don't fret. Unless you're going into the publishing industry. A course I strongly advise against). Yes, memory of sailing in Dún Laoghaire is akin to one of those elaborate dropped capital letters so popular in older books. Or indeed in the Book of Kells. Akin, yes, akin because those decorations and florishes bear little relationship to the words that follow. Or to the meaning of the words that follow. They're just there as a punctuation. Enjoy this, they urge, there's something else coming down the tracks.

Words borrow the next. And as I type the word *tracks* I realise that I did not hurtle all the way down from Killiney with Dairine on my crossbar. OK I did hurtle down the first part of the Killiney Road. To the crossroads at the top of Albert Road. Crossroads? Yes, no roundabout then, we're going back a bit here. I hurtled down as far as the crossroads and the momentum carried me all the way on to Glenageary bridge. So that was ok so. That was the easy bit, now for the tricky. The route from there to the West Pier was along the metals. Beside the railway *tracks*. And there surely is a downhill gradient along the metals, but believe you me they seemed very flat to a bronchitic boy on a bike. Particularly a bronchitic boy with a largish female on the crossbar. But needs must, and a teenage boy will put up with a lot to get into close contact with female flesh. It's nature's way.

I cycled along the metals as far as they went, to the bottom of Marine Road. Then along Crofton Road to the bridge over the railway leading down to the Coal Harbour. Over that and then along the pathway to the West Pier. Quite a way, really. And then there at the back of the West Pier which always smelled of soap because of the soap factory Dairine would hop off the crossbar and go about her business. I don't recall her ever saying thanks. But I suppose she reckoned that three or four miles of her breasts against my arm was thanks enough.

I'd park my bike with the other bikes against the fence. Bikes were the thing really, lots of bikes. Except for Gary Hooper who had a motor scooter and a brother who was a solicitor and a girlfriend called Philippa Feddis. Her father Matt played in jazz bands round the town. With Johnny Wadham who lived beside my granny in Dalkey. We were a small close knit community!

Another exception from the world of bicycles was the Jewish boy, he had a motor bike. A low powered motorbike, but a motorbike nonetheless. We tended not to pay much attention to Gary Hooper's motor scooter because those yokes were ubiquitous, even though we didn't know the word. But the Jewish boy's motorbike was something else. It had an exotic and interesting quality. And invariably groups of teenagers would cluster around it, admiring. And he'd sit astride, smiling in a nerdy fashion.

Then we'd all go sailing.

There were no particular clothes to wear in those days, no particular sailing gear. Yes there were yellow oilskins, but they were cumbersome in a dinghy. So we just wore rough clothes and tennis shoes. Sneakers in modern parlance. And yes we did wear lifejackets. But of the type that could either drown you or make you look like a victim of the Titanic. They would float you yes, but there is very little point in floating if you can't get your face out of the water. Lifejackets were dangerous in dinghies. If you capsized going about then the sail could come back down over you. The lifejacket would bob you up against the sail, you wouldn't be able to dive down to escape.

It was a horror frequently discussed.

I didn't have my own boat, but I sailed one of the club boats or *Red Shoes*, a dinghy owned by Johnnie Walker. A solicitor, he'd bought it for his daughter Pauline. (Being a mere travelling salesman, my father hadn't bought me anything except the bike). Pauline was dark and nice and she wore very short shorts and had lovely thighs. A connection there no doubt. But ours was strictly a professional relationship. I was the helmsman and she was the crew. I was the helmsman because Johnnie Walker wanted a return on his investment in the shape of winning races. Which I did. Because I was really very good. And should've gone on to the Olympics really. Yes there's a bitterness there. Mind you in adulthood I also should've won the Booker Prize. The bitterness continues.

So, after winning a race, it was all uphill. Back to Killiney. While downhill was awhirl with potential and enthusiasm, uphill was a bit of trudge. And coming home from sailing one was usually wet. It was tough and tedious and we were tired. A refreshment stop would be made, maybe along the metals at that shop on Eden Road. It's now a crèche. And people who were not born when I cycled past that way leave their babies in. One can sense a worry of mortgage and traffic on their minds. They'd best be thinking something else but of course they won't. We don't. We never do.

We'd stop there for Tayto crisps and other nutritious stuff. Or maybe we wouldn't, we'd cycle on to the shop at Glenageary Bridge. Mr O'Rourke's. And we'd stop there for crisps and other nutritious stuff. It was a mood thing. And we wouldn't know which shop we were going to stop at until we actually did stop. Just as now in my job I never know quite what I'm going to write until I do write. I know I'm going to write x thousand words, because I need to eat. But what precise form those x thousand words will take…well…lap of gods' stuff.

Indeed, I have often sat down to write with something in the mind, something particular. An article, a blog, a book…and then after a hundred words or so I have found myself writing something completely different. And it's a mystery where that difference comes from. But then there's lots of mysteries in this writing game. (Not least the wonderment as to why many Irish writers think they can write.) But this piece here, no mystery as to its origins. An hour before I started work I read a death notice on the internet.

FREEDMAN, Dr. John - November 24, 2011, slipped away peacefully, in his 97th year, at Bloomfield. Dearly loved husband of the late Doreen, wonderful much loved father of Derek, father-in-law of Gillian, grandfather of Andrew and Michael great-grandfather of Mia. He had time for everybody, and basks in the great affection of his friends and many patients, who were his friends. Funeral took place on Thursday November 24, 2011 at Dolphin's Barn.

John and Doreen Freedman, yes, that was their names, those loving Jewish parents, standing on the wall at the back of the West Pier. *Alov hasholom*. Yes, that was them. Watching their son Derek in his boat. I google him just now. Yes, their son the doctor. And more than that, their son the distinguished genito-urinary consultant. Specialist in sexually transmitted diseases. I thought yes, I should get in touch. But he might invite me round to talk of old times. Problem here. The internet shows me that his Ranelagh house seems to be contiguous with his clinic. His sexually transmitted diseases clinic. And I don't really want to be seen going up those steps. So I'll just say hi from here.

Hi Derek.

So, tell me.

How do you get into that specialization?

Canoes

OUR FAMILY PRAM HAD A BASEMENT. In that if one removed the baby, one came across a hatch. By lifting this hatch one had access to the basement area, a large curved space for carrying groceries and necessities back from the shops. I'm not at all sure if my mother ever used it for that purpose, and in no way recall ever being lifted out while she loaded up. Though I do remember going around in the pram. My sister had done likewise before me. It was a fairly huge contraption. *Silver Cross*, I reckon, highly polished like a custom coached Rolls Royce. And with a certain amount of chrome.

In time our younger siblings had more modern push chairs, prototype buggies. Sort of Model T Ford buggies, nothing like the one I recently bought for my daughter's baby in famous Tony Kealy's of Coolock. Rephrase that...nothing like the one my daughter recently bought for her baby in Tony Kealy's of Coolock, myself merely tagging along as technical advisor. I know my prams.

After my older sister and I (she won't like that word *older*), after our babyhood the Silver Cross was consigned to the garage, and storage. Just in case the Edwardian way of life came back into fashion. It didn't. The pram had gone into that category of storage where leftovers from a meal are put in the fridge to be thrown out later. A half way house sort of storage, a just-in-case. It was never used again but the just-in-case solution did prove fortuitous.

Because, around the age of sixteen I built a canoe and the pram came into its own...albeit in a different role. It was just as if, for example, my mother and (older) sister had decided that they wanted to sell bananas in Camden Street, the pram would also have come into its own. Truth is, it was useless as a baby vehicle. Particularly around Killiney and Dalkey, very hilly locations. Essentially it was designed for the flat, and was meant to have a crisply uniformed nanny at the handle, wearing black stockings and sensible shoes and...oh but let's not get into her uniform. Enough to say it was designed for that particular fantasy nanny...I have a range of fantasy nannies to choose from...but our Silver Cross was just for her, to push along through Kensington Palace Gardens. How and ever, in Dublin terms its purpose was for flogging bananas. That, or being converted into a bicycle trailer for transporting canoes.

I dismantled it and reassembled it for that latter purpose. Essentially I was after the wheels and chassis but due to technicalties the finished trailer did come along with a certain amount of chrome and extraneous bling. All in all, it was pretty flash, which is a lot more than can be said for my first canoe. A rudimentary craft, I designed it myself. And that, as the saying has it, was my first mistake. It was woegeous. But of course I didn't know that at the time. To me it looked terrific. Almost as impressive as my brylcreamed quiff and pointy shoes.

I loaded it on to the trailer, attached the trailer to the bike and set off. It wasn't easy, because it was downhill to the sea from my house and the trailer kept catching up on the bike. I found I had to go faster and faster to avoid being overtaken. But, on the positive side, I realised it'd be easier coming back up. And designed in my mind a rigid coupling between bike and trailer which would at a later date solve the downhill problem. These technical breakthroughs need tweaking.

The prototype canoe was launched at the slipway by the East Pier. This was once the launching spot for Dún Laoghaire lifeboats, and thus a very appropriate place to launch that particular canoe. Worried looking watery harbour types gathered around me as I removed it from its pram...I mean its trailer. They looked at the canoe. They looked at each other. They looked at me.

"You're not going out in that."

"Sure I am."

"Where are you going?

"Just so far as the harbour mouth."

They looked at the far off harbour mouth. They looked at the canoe. They looked at each other. They looked at me.

"It doesn't seem very safe," said one.

"Pah," I said, unloading. What did they know, those old watery types? Just because they'd spent a lifetime around ships and sailing round the Horn before the mast in howling storms, what did they know?

I slid the canoe into the water, jumped in and headed off. But not for long. Five to ten yards, just about that. The vessel had an inherent instability and capsized. I stood up to my waist in the water and then dragged it back up the slipway.

"Just testing," I said to the watery types, "needs a few modifications."

"Needs a keel," said one watery type.

"Those hard chines and flat bottom, need a keel if you're going to have hard chines and a flat bottom."

"Canoes don't have keels" I told him.

"They don't have flat bottoms either. They need round bottoms."

"My missus needs one of those" said another watery type. And they all laughed, and went about their business.

Hah, I thought, what do they know, silly old buggers.

Yes it was great to be sixteen, knowing everything.

I put the canoe back up on the trailer/pram, hitched it to the bicycle and cycled back up to Killiney. There I unloaded, unhitched the trailer, changed my clothes... and cycled right back to Dún Laoghaire. This time to the Library. And there I borrowed a book of how-to-build-canoes, with fold out plans and diagrams at the back.

I took the book home and studied it. I was tempted to tear the plans out of the back of the library book, like who's to know?

I resisted the temptation, but not from any inner sense of right and wrong, of ethics and morality, and awareness of the social compact. I didn't do any of that stuff then. Not sure if things have changed much either as regards my inner sense of right and wrong, of ethics and morality, and awareness of the social compact. I don't tend to let fancy words and concepts stand between myself and survival. God and I have an understanding. So long as I do His work, He lets me cut some corners. But anyway back then I resisted the temptation to rip up the book because it was out on my mother's library tickets and, like the prospect of imminent execution, the fear of an imminent mother concentrates the mind. I got greaseproof paper from the kitchen and carefully traced the plans. (Mr Xerox was still working on his photocopying machine in those days.)

Over the next week or so I got in supplies. I cycled down to Murdoch's in Park Road and bought long slender laths of wood. And tied them to the crossbar and cycled back, the bunch of laths protruding front and back like the lance on a jousting horse. I also bought a sheet of ply, but couldn't take that on the bike and arranged delivery. And it came a few days later in Murdoch's little van. A little van done up to look like a miniature oil tanker. They used it to deliver Esso Blue paraffin around the suburbs. They were the local Esso Blee Doolers, or so they said on the advertising jingles. Your local Esso Blee Dooler.

Saatchi and Saatchi, eat your heart out.

I set to work. It wasn't easy, I had no access to any power tools whatsoever, my father wasn't into DIY. I never actually saw him lift a hammer. Or a paintbrush. My mother did all that. Without her that house would have been a crypt. Actually even with her it was a bit of a crypt, big and draughty and cold. But we did have maids. Not in canoe building days when I was sixteen, times had changed by then, but when a small child. Pity we didn't have maids when I was sixteen. I really need the memory of some seduction. The young master and the peasant girl from County Carlow, that stuff. Downton Abbey stuff. She sits on the bed in the maid's room...yes there was a maid's room...and she rolls down a stocking with a County Carlow smile. Her thigh is very white. Particularly because it's darkening on a winter afternoon. And the house is empty except for us. Yes, that precise stuff. A writer really needs that memory. But it's missing from my portfolio. Pity. Missing because by the time I was sixteen the maid's room, whilst still called the maid's room, was empty, and its bed likewise. No Carlow thighs nor Carlow breasts behind that panelled door. Pity, damn pity. But I did build a model plane in there, laying it out on the lino floor where once the maid's pretty little Carlow feet had padded bare. Yes she had lino whilst we had carpets. (Those sociological details did not escape me). The model plane had an elastic motor to the propeller. I wound it up and launched it from the window. Went down to our garden or to the neighbours' the Nolans' garden, depending on wind conditions, retrieved it and launched it again from the window.

This got very boring after awhile.

I brought it to the window one more time, wound it up, set light to the tail, and launched it. In a ball of flame it careered across the garden. Landed in a bush and set fire to it. My mother said what the hell do you think you're doing, you could have set fire to Ballinclea Heights.

I told her the plane wouldn't have flown that far..

She said I'm going to have to have a word with your father.

Happy days. And if I had set fire to Ballinclea Heights, all the happier. That is and always was one depressing housing estate. One bad place. Went into decay and marriage-collapse-mode almost as soon as built. Bad architecture or simple bad vibes from restless spirits of the earth?

Maybe a combination. But no matter, the new canoe, the professionally designed canoe, that was a complete success.

It launched successfully, and I spent a week or so paddling round Dún Laoghaire Harbour. In those days it was still interesting. There were little creeks and mini harbours, and hidden slipways. But interesting or not it soon got pretty damn boring. And I suppose I could have set fire to the canoe and pushed it out to sea in a Viking funeral scenario, but I didn't. Because the new canoe had created interest among the sixteen year old boy demographic of the borough. And they asked me where I got it, and I told them I'd built it. And some of them asked would I build one for them? And I did. And thus began my canoe building business. I built canoes and sold them far and wide. Well, far and wide if far was Sandycove and wide was Blackrock, that sort of orbit. Remember some of my sales. In Sandycove I sold to a boy who grew up to become an Aer Lingus pilot and marry Patricia Cullen of Dalkey. Can't remember his name, tend to remember the females better. She was nice, and very. Her brother Peter and Tony Macken and myself went hurtling round in cars. The world of letters is lucky I'm still alive. But I survived. Unlike Patricia who never came out on those car driving skites, stayed safely at home in her father's Colamore Hotel. But has died since, quite young. Life is arbitrary and cruel, death haphazard.

That was the Sandycove sale, and there were others all along the coastline, the names of purchasers forgotten. But in Blackrock remembered. There I sold a canoe to young Campbell of the Campbell shop which used be around the corner from Meaneys. Not that Meaneys is there anymore so such directions are useless. He had a sister who became a politician. But that's sisters for you.

Never knew that particular sister. Pity really, because she was not just a sister, she became Nuala Fennell, a politician I admired. And that takes some doing. Strange we never met, because I did collect sisters of boys I dealt with.

Useful things, sisters. Well, other people's sisters. Though in later years my (older) sister in London did come in useful, for me meeting-certain-women-wise. I'll say no more, stay schtum. But still she'll look at me through narrowed eyes. Enough to note that one was English, one Irish, and one Indian. London is a cosmopolitan city. But whatever, back earlier it was other people's sisters who were very important in the scheme of things to a boy on a bicycle.

Around this time I seemed to have been hanging round with Cluny Convent girls. They wore blue, a nice cool colour for a teenage girl. And we gathered, teenage boys and girls in Avondale Road near the school gates. The girls clustered round the very beautiful Jill Clancey like they hoped something would rub off. But they were all pretty attractive anyway...to a boy on a bicycle! And there on their bikes they looked like they'd cycled from directly out of a Betjeman poem. Well to me they did because I read poetry. To the rest of the guys I suppose they just looked like girls. But to me...different. Leggy and tousled. And the sun shone on their legs and their hair tossed in summery breeze. That sort of scene. And I suppose it was some compensation for not having a County Carlow peasant girl back in the house. Not a complete compensation of course, but life is a mirror reflecting mirrors, and we must do with the image to hand.

Avondale Road was interesting. Which I know may sound absurd to the residents there, in these the moody mornings of their mortgages, and their evenings of despair. But back then it had only recently been built, and there were still pockets of farmland around. And lanes through fields of grain to cycle down. It was all incomplete, the jigsaw where two worlds meet. Rural and suburban, old and new. And there was still some building going on in Avondale Road itself. This to me became the focus of my interest. Well that and Mary Finnegan's legs as she cycled along beside me. Yes that same Mary now a Dublin journalist whom I worshipped from afar. And quite close up sometimes too.

I was interested in the building activities because I myself was a businessman, my business building canoes. And, as a businessman, an entrepreur, a sole trader, a member of the SME class, I had many responsibilities. And my worries were many, mostly centred round profit margins, and the price of materials down in Murdoch's, all that.

I cycled along with Mary Finnegan. I looked at her legs. And I looked at the half built houses around us. Now here's the thing. Whilst a woman's legs create problems in parallel to the solutions offered, half built houses can create stand alone solutions. As in building materials going a-begging. I cycled along, Mary's legs whirling round to a background of building materials. And I was thoughtful. And it would be nice to record that I decided to marry Mary Finnegan, and move into one of those little bungalows, and raise a family. But I didn't, didn't decide to marry her, which is probably just as well for both of us. But it must be said that when I meet up with her now there are regrets...a few. Which phrase, yes, it is a lyric from a schmaltzy song.

Instead of deciding to marry Mary Finnegan I decided to steal building materials for my canoes from the sites in Avondale Road. And that very night, in dead of dark, I cycled back to Avondale Road. And a bat swooped over my head as if to set a scene. It really did, there were bats in the old Belton's barns. And an unknown animal screeched in the middle distance. Was that a cat? Perhaps, let's hope. (Though my editor tells me now that it was a fox, a female fox being rogered, they screech like that. Rogered? His phrase, not mine, I write, he edits. But how do editors know these things? I don't know these things.)

I loaded up the bike with suitable lengths of timber, and cycled back. And thereafter once a week or so I would do the same. My finances improved, dramatically. I could now afford to take my girlfriend to the Pav. I could afford to buy beer and sit in Walter's with my mates. Granted, I couldn't afford to marry Mary Finnegan.

No, there were things I could afford and things I couldn't.

I just had to grin and bear it.

I was a businessman and self sufficient.

Man of the world.

Grinning. And bearing it.

Walters

THE TABLE WHERE I SAT was made from the support of an old industrial sewing machine, its ironwork said *Singer* and the foot pedal was still attached. I sat there, swinging it back and forth. And decided I was a seamstress, an old worn woman, a lifetime in the garment trade. Back and forth, swinging, my legs, back and forth. Making skirts and waistcoats. It came to me easy, because my mother's family were tailors, going back the generations. It's in the dna. So I sat there easy, swinging that pedal and drinking my bottle of Guinness. Walters was a desperate pub with one advantage… they didn't care if I was sixteen or sixty.

I was sixteen. And whatever about Walters, I cared. So I decided not to be an old worn woman seamstress. I decided to be a young girl, an apprentice at the trade, yes that would suit me better. Much better. I swung the pedal back and forth. Working out who I was and what I looked like. No bother with those questions really. Because for certain I was very pretty, and for certain intelligent. Though rather uneducated, which was a pity. Because I did have potential for a better way of life, something more satisfying than being a seamstress. But it was not to be. There was many of us in the family. My father had left on the mailboat, to England for work. And yes he did find work, and at first he sent money back to my mother. But then he found another woman, and the money tailed off, and we lost contact. And so there was only my mother and I, to support the younger children. Worse than that, there was really only myself. Because my mother had....polio? No. Typhoid? No, maybe not. Glaucoma, yes, glaucoma, my mother had glaucoma. And she could no longer work. She needed the eyesight because she had actually been a seamstress herself. But she did manage to get me a job in the factory as an apprentice. And so here I sat, swinging the pedal back and forth.

I was very pretty. But then, I wasn't going to sit in Walters being a plain girl. No way, what would be the point? I was very pretty and I had good big breasts. To hell with being flat chested. And...and I had nice legs. Though they were under the table and no-one could see them. But...but maybe they could see them through the open ironwork that said *Singer*? Maybe. And just in case I hitched my dress up a little to show a little knee.

I sipped my Guinness.

Guinness? What am I talking about here?

I sipped my Babycham. And thought about my situation. So here I am, I thought. Pretty. And busty. And showing a bit of knee. But alone, not a soul paying a blind bit of attention to me. Shit. Men! Men-who-needs-them! Jesus would you look at the fuckers. Sitting there along the bar. Discussing horses. And football. Or staring into space.

But what else was new? A lot of people actually spent a lot of time in Walters staring into space. As if waiting for the invention of television. Oh yes of course television had been invented, but it hadn't penetrated into Walters bar just yet. And as for Sky, that was for clouds, sometimes, and stars other.

A lot of things hadn't penetrated into Walters Bar just yet. Civilisation being one of the main elements. It was rough. The customers were rough. And there was a thuggish element who'd pick fights. They went by surnames, to avoid. McGovern. Hudson, and McCoy. Which written down like that now reads like a trio of gunslingers riding into a wild west town. But I suppose in these days terms they weren't that bad, they'd only beat you up, not stamp on your head or stab you like the modern manifestation of their kind. Old men now, McGovern. Hudson, and McCoy. I should seek them out and push them off their walking frames. But I can't do that to the ferocious Christy Tate, dead now. A stuttering bar brawling bloke from Eden Villas. Though the useful thing about that stutter was it gave a guy an out. Christy would take so long to say fff-f-f-f-fuck you jjj-j-j-j-just ffff-f-f-f-fuck you that there was time to get out of the line of fire. He was goodlooking, charming and likeable. Until he smashed a barstool over your head.

For Lordssakes...

I really don't know what a pretty young girl like myself was doing in a place like that at all. Perhaps because it was the only bar in Dún Laoghaire that would serve a sixteen year old? Precisely, and so myself and my friends all went there. But not tonight. None of my friends were in. Probably just as well. Not sure how they would've dealt with me being pretty, busty, short skirted. Sexual ambivalence was kept pretty much low key in our circle. In any event, they hadn't turned up, it was that sort of night. I hadn't even turned up myself. Because I wasn't me. Tonight I was a girl, and pensive. And Walters was empty apart from the few usual suspects along the bar...and apart from me, this pretty young girl looking down at her Guinness on the table.

Fuckit no, her bottle of Babycham on the table.

I reached out to the glass. I had pale and well formed fingers, I noted. And I needed them, their slenderness. Because things were moving fast here now and I decided that the big tits I'd given myself were rather coarse and crass, and I needed elegant fingers to create a balance, bring on something more delicate, refined. Just to balance, I didn't want to give up the crass tits, no, I liked the weight of them, not to mention the taut elasticity of the flesh, but I did need something to draw attention elsewhere. Something delicate. To demonstrate a different aspect of my persona. Elegant slender fingers were just the thing. On the button. Who's going to look at my silly big knockers when there were elegant slender fingers to admire? Yes, this woman thing...it's all about the multiple layers and facets. If a woman were pastry she should be filo.

Flakey even. Stodgy never.

(Jesus where is an editor when I need one?)

I looked at my delicate fingers and was suddenly sorry that I had painted those nails scarlet. The horror, and the ladylike in me screeched, but silently. Quickly I pulled my hand back, folding it into a fist so the scarlet would not flash like brakelights and give out the wrong impression. Not that it was easy to give out any impression at all, no-one was looking at me. I dug into my handbag among bottles and pots and lotions and potions. And quickly repainted my nails a more subtle colour. The smell of it. You can sniff that stuff to get a high. But what teenage boy needs a high when he's sitting in Walters with heavy breasts and painting his nails a shade of…coral…yes. Coral. A milky pinky white, something like one sees at the bottom of an icecream sundae glass. That half spoon of liquid you can never quite get out.

Feeling better now.

I reached out again and raised the wine to my lips and sipped. Delicately. As if I knew about wine but wasn't saying. Then almost immediately I thought oh shit. Oh shit oh shit. My lips are lipsticked to match those scarlet nails ! My scarlet nails which I have just repainted coral. I can't have that. I'm just in bits, colourwise, image wise, I'm all over the place. Nothing for it but…so I quickly put the wineglass back down on the table and reached into the bag again, rummaged among lipsticks. There were lots of lipsticks in there because…because? Yes yes yes I said yes. Because as well as being an apprentice seamstress I was a professional shoplifter and stole small items to sell to the other girls in the garment factory at a significant discount to shop prices. I was never caught. That innocent air about me.

I repainted my lips a more appropriate and ladylike colour, and glossed them shiny. I pouted at the small cosmetic mirror which I had stolen earlier in Mahoney and Ennis Pharmacy at the top of Marine Road… and I was very pleased indeed. Very pleased. But perhaps…maybe I was looking a bit bland now that the scarlet lipstick was gone. Yes, no maybe about it, a bit bland. Back into the bag again. Mascara, eye shadow. I did my eyes. The small cosmetic mirror told me that was better. Perhaps a bit heavy on the eye shadow, as if I had a tragic past or a sexy future but… just leave it be. I left it be and put everything back into the bag…which I had stolen a few weeks back in McCullaghs up the town.

I put the bag beside me on the bench.

Bench, yes. Not a banquette as they call them in modern pubs.

Walters did benches, wooden ones. Nothing velveteen. The slats were hard against my thighs. But hard against my thighs was good. I could take it. I sipped my former Guinness which, like some female and disorientated Christ, I had turned into wine. It had started off as Babycham but was now a passable Sauvignon Blanc. A person develops a palate.

I crossed my legs, to show a bit of ladylike thigh. Not that the backs along the bar would see the bit of ladylike thigh, but if there were someone sitting further up the bench, he would. I glanced surreptitiously further up the bench. There was no-one sitting further up the bench. I glanced surreptitiously in the other direction, down towards the door. And yes there was, there was there was there was someone sitting there.

A man. A bit old, yes. But still a man. Though smoking a pipe. Which was a downer. But he wasn't personally on fire, so remained passable. I recrossed my legs, the other over the other. So that the ladylike thigh was revealed in his direction.

The older man with the pipe ignored me. No, he didn't ignore me, to ignore one has to see first. He didn't see me. My lipstick. My eyeshadow. My seductive thigh. My fulsome breasts in profile proud and young and thrusting, none of that. He saw a sixteen year old teenage boy drinking a bottle of Guinness.

Blind bastard, I thought.

Blind blind bastard, bastards, the lot of them, I'm out of here.

I finished my wine and put the glass back on the table. With a finality, like it was a hand of cards in a game I couldn't win. A game I couldn't win no matter how hard I played. No matter how skilled or cunning, it was the dealer dealt the cards.

I stood up, and no-one noticed me. And I didn't even leave an empty seat behind me, because no-one noticed the emptiness either. They didn't even seem to see me reflected in the mirror behind the bar, which was strange. Because I could see myself there. A sixteen year old seamstress and shoplifter, walking towards the door. Strange, strange they couldn't see me. And I thought of vampires. Vampires have no reflections in the mirror. They can't even see themselves. So was I some kind of super vampire, invisible to all except myself?

Hard to tell, hard to tell.

I walked up Georges Street. It was late and dark and quiet and quietly raining. And my high heels clicked like the clock in a funeral parlour when the mourners had gone home. A car pulled up alongside and the driver entered into discussion and negotiation. Because yes as well as being a seamstress and a shoplifter the girl in me was a prostitute too. She was multifaceted. The girl in me was more or less everything a woman could be, she just hadn't quite made up her mind. What part of herself to accept, what to reject. I leant in his window to be polite, it's important in business. We chatted some, but I was only being polite.

I walked on.

Walked on past Mr Doyle the shoemakers. And thought of his pretty daughter Gay. And her boyfriend Gary Keogh. And didn't know the future, hers or mine. Didn't know that I'd meet her later in South Africa. In Durban. That we'd drink guava juice together, and talk of Dún Laoghaire. But how should or could I know? All that was in the far future, and I just didn't know. And I didn't know that even further, much much later in the far far future I'd read about Gary throwing eggs at the directors of Allied Irish Banks. Yes all those futures were there…but I didn't know them. Didn't know that I passed the shop where Shirley would run a secretarial agency in years to come, years far in the future. Shirley Egan. Her father had a Coco Cola franchise. As teenagers we thought that very impressive. She married Peter Cullen. And his father owned the Colamore Hotel in Dalkey. The marriage didn't last. He left her. Started a sweet factory. All that in the far far future which I didn't know.

I walked on, on in that far past which I know quite well, too well?

Maybe. I walked on past Marchbank and Agnew, protestant electrical suppliers. And I said to myself just as well it's closed and dark. Mr Marchbank and Mr Agnew wouldn't like to see me walking past their window. In my high heels. Short skirt. And with my tumble of hair and my heavy breasts.

Protestants…they like their whores hidden.

I had left the bike chained to the railings of that little shop next Sweeneys Auctioneers. *Your Key to House Purchase*. Chained to that little shop which sold fowl and rabbits. A narrow shop, barely wider than it's own front door. The owner Mr Daly wore a rubbery apron to his ankles, no doubt bloody things went on out back. He decorated the outside frame of his door with produce. Pheasants in season, hanging there like hats abandoned at a wedding when the night moves on. And rabbits, always rabbits, rabbits throughout the year. Right there, outside his door. As an enticement to customers and flies. But now the shop was closed and the rabbits gone inside. I could see them hanging in there in the dark. Boy rabbits, girl rabbits. You wouldn't know the difference in the gloom. Or in a stew either. You skin a rabbit like taking off a sock. And whether it's a girl rabbit or a boy rabbit the skin just peels away the same, easily.

I unchained the bike. My high heels were much too high for cycling so I kicked them off. And looked at them there at the edge of the road where the water runs to its drain. One shoe standing, the other lying beside. And I smiled at the way they had fallen. And I left them there in George's Street and cycled home.

Barefoot in a darkness.

Young Ladies

NOT MANY PEOPLE can say this. But the grandfather of my teenage girlfriend invented the pneumatic tyre. Well, the grandfather of *one* of my teenage girlfriends. There were a few. In those years it's the same love, spread thinly so's to cover every available option. I'm not even sure how long the girl whose grandfather invented the pneumatic tyre actually was my teenage girlfriend. Maybe only one summer. And a winter. Yes definitely at least one summer, and one winter. Must've been, because I remember summer things with her, and winter things as well. So it was a balanced love affair. The length of time is immaterial. It's all a question of quality, not quantity. And even if it were for only one day that she was my girlfriend…her grandfather did still invent the pneumatic tyre. That can't be taken away from him. And nor in fact can it be taken away from me. As her boyfriend I was up there with the greats. These things rub off.

It gets better.

The father of the cousin of my girlfriend (whose grandfather invented the pneumatic tyre) owned Arnotts Department Store. More or less. Yes, he did share ownership with some other members of the family, it being a family business. And one of those other members of the family was the mother of my girlfriend (whose grandfather invented the pneumatic tyre). So the links to the ownership of Arnotts were both complex and financially satisfying. But who's counting anyway? Any shares in the ownership of Dublin's largest department store are not to be sneezed at. We're not talking a Centra in Killester here.

Bottom line?

I was now moving among rich and respectable people.

Solid as inherited furniture.

Gentry.

Young ladies.

This connection (with the girl whose etcetera etcetera) brought me back to my roots, my true place in the social order. Because my own background was also in the upper middle classes. In fact we hovered close to titled folks. But we had fallen, and were now quite poor. However I did have good blood and breeding. And the father of my teenage girlfriend, who's own father had invented the pneumatic tyre, accepted me. Living in Dalkey he knew my seed and breed. And the great mansion where my mother had been born. So he accepted me socially. Financially I'm none too sure. I was to learn in later years that he was notoriously tight, and in recent times an old man in Killiney Golf Club told me he would stay out on the course all night, with a flashlight, looking for his lost ball from a morning game. A story no doubt with its roots in a joke in the bar... but the roots of jokes?

No matter. He accepted me socially and no doubt he consoled himself financially by the awareness that the affair would pass. And his daughter would not marry a penniless Roman Catholic oik.

Yes, these people were Protestants. And not only that, the man who invented the pneumatic tyre came from Belfast. So these people were Protestants from Belfast. Say no more. We're all Irish now. Cross border institutions. Peace process. Bedding down. Martin McGuinness. Say no more. Cut to the chase. And hey, my own father was a Protestant. And if ecumenism is to have any meaning...all that.

The girlfriend lived in Dalkey, in a large and stately house near Bulloch Harbour. Beulah was its name, and probably still is, and it was a totally suitable place for the granddaughter of the man who invented the pneumatic tyre. I would cycle down to see her. And, if she still lived there, I would cycle off to see her this very moment. Yes, I'd be off. I'd pump up the (pneumatic) tyres on a bike and head right off. (Unless the hip or knee was playing up more than usual.) I would cycle right down there to see her because she was very beautiful. With, I imagine, the sort of beauty that has survived these long decades. The sort of beauty that has not only survived, but has matured, and deepened, and become meaningful in the eternal scheme of things.

A blonde of the fairest, almost white, she had features fragile and delicately drawn. She was slender, but shapely, and if I remember any more I'll weep into this keyboard, so that's quite enough. Though it must be added that she was not at all personally fragile herself, as tough as nails in fact, and perhaps even hard, but her disguise as a gentle fragile girl was much appreciated.

Much. Appreciated.

She and her cousin attended *Rathdown School*, as weekly boarders. Though called *Hillcourt* then, the school was much the same as now. Why they were boarders I cannot fathom, the school being merely a mile or two from each of their homes. Perhaps they had been sent away to keep them out of the clutches of Roman Catholic oiks such as myself?

If so, it did not work.

It was decided by my friend David and I to visit these girls in their school.

At dead of night we cycled there.

The arrangement was prior, and the girls opened a window of their dormitory. We were discussing things generally when things went pear shaped, pear shaped in the shape of flashing blue lights coming up the drive. Someone had spotted us and had alerted the law and order.

That part of the Rathdown building is an old house with a semi basement all around. David and I ran around this to escape at the back.

Bad move. The cops split up, so that one was running in one direction around the house, the other in the other. And so we ran into their arms and were hauled off to Dún Laoghaire Police Station.

"What about my bike?" I asked in the back of the police car.

"You've more to worry than your bike" was the reply.

But as it turned out I didn't. The arresting guard turned out to be the husband of the owner of Clerys shop in the holla in Glasthule. And the owner of Clerys shop in the holla in Glasthule was a customer of my father, who was a travelling salesman, in cigarettes. Travelling salesmen travelled *in* things. My father in fact had several travelling salesman jokes playing on this usage. Like so and so who travelled in women's underwear. That sort of joke.

You had to be there.

Words were had in ears. I was released without charge, as was my friend David. He piggybacking on my connections and influence among the shopkeeping/Garda community. Which goes to show, it's all about who you're arrested with. Anyway, we were released with severe remonstrations as to future behaviour. And to stay away from Hillcourt School.

I didn't.

A day or so later I went down there and presented myself to a functionary. She was thin and disapproving. I suppose it was a long time since anyone climbed through her window.

"I've come to collect my bicycle" I told her.

"Well you'll have to speak to Miss Mew" I was told.

"Miss Mew?"

"Miss Stella Mew, she's the headmistress."

I spoke to Miss Mew. She was formidable, pronounced in the French manner. Even if one thought it, she wasn't the sort of Stella with whom one would make jokes about the eponymous cinema in Rathmines.

"I've come to collect my bicycle," I told her.

"Well you're not getting your bicycle until you apologise."

"For what?"

"For trespass and invading the privacy of the girls."

"But the girls…" I started.

"Don't but the girls me," said Miss Stella Mew. "And if you were a gentleman you would not attempt to blame innocent young ladies for your outrageous behaviour."

"I'm just saying…"

"Well don't, or you'll never see your bicycle again."

I apologised. I retrieved the bike and cycled down the drive. My fame had gone before me. There was some kind of hockey practice on and gaggles of girls pointed and chortled as I passed. This was my perp walk, the pedal power version. Surrounded not by papparazzi but by cartoons come alive. Ronald Searle cartoons. Those weird dark stockinged spider-legged short skirted schoolgirls, they ranged from the pre-pubescent to the fulsomely nubile. And Hillcourt schoolgirls did the fulsomely nubile well. The modern Rathdown version surely still do, even with that change of name. But that factor was far from my thoughts. Cycling down that avenue then they were all equally evil to my mind. It was a scene something between St Trinian's and Japanese anime pornography. Terrible.

I cycled out the gate and along the Glenageary Road. Thinking *innocent young ladies*, and adding *hah!* Or muttering *innocent young ladies my arse.*

A learning curve. But the thing about learning curves is that they lead around corners, and things change. And so we grew older, the granddaughter of the man who invented the pneumatic tyre and I. But maybe not together. Not enough anyway. Things petered out. The back row of the Pav cinema was no longer enough to bring our separate needs together. And the affair ended in a drama on Whiterock Beach.

It was a moonlit night, I well remember.

And that's a sentence that I never thought I'd write. But that wall is ready for all writers to hit. And it really was, a moonlit night. A full moon with that path of moonlight across the water, that photographer's cliché, that path so clearly defined you might try walking there. Yes I remember that. And I well remember more. But will tell no more about it. Yes I would go down there some other moonlit night, and write the story on the sand, just for the hell of it. But only if the tide were coming in. Because, contrary to the opinion of Miss Stella Mew, I am a gentleman and do respect the dignity and privacy of women. And yes that does sound frightfully pompous and old fashioned. It comes from the same old school as standing aside for a woman at the opening of a door. Pompous and old fashioned and even patronising, probably sexist.

Well so be it.

Sticks and stones etcetera.

And words will never hurt me.

Except the ones I write myself.

The Gatekeeper

THERE'S A GHOST in an hotel in South Africa, the Nottingham Road Hotel. I know her well. But who she is and why she's there I do not rightly know. But one thing I do know is that the same hotel haunts me, because I've been writing a novel by that name for several years. *The Nottingham Road Hotel.* But I may not finish it. And I suppose that adds up to a haunting of another kind. No doubt there's a reason for that, for not finishing a book. Just as, perhaps, there once was a reason for starting the damn thing in the first place.

But then there's lots of books, finished and unfinished. And I'd just finished this particular one and was feeling pretty good about myself… and then the ghost from South Africa came to me in a dream. And she said about my name. And I said what, what about your name?

"I don't think you should use it in that book."

"Why, for godsakes, everyone knows your name, everyone in Nottingham Road anyway."

"It's not for my sake, but that woman, that woman in Ireland who shares my name, you write about her."

"Jesus woman, it was a long long time ago, who's to know and who's

91

to care?"

"I care," said the ghost from Nottingham Road, "so take out my name. You can use the initial. What difference does it make if no-one cares or no-one knows?"

Well it makes a bloody difference to the editor and the typesetter and the designer, I told her, they're going to be rightly pissed off. And at that the ghost laughed in my dream. Best piss them off than me, she said.

And I lay there listening to her laughter fade.

I was in my Italian village that month, and her laughter faded into the sound of morning poultry, and the putter of motorscooters passing. And I got up and wrote...rewrote...these words.

So, her name is C, that ghost.

But long before I lived in Africa, and long before I knew there was a ghost by that name in a particular building, long before all that I knew a girl called C in Dún Laoghaire. I met her at the funfair on Victoria Wharf.

Victoria Wharf?

It's buried under the car ferry terminal complex. There's a plaza with serpentine seats finished in blue mosaic, some designer's big day. Backpackers sit there, waiting for ferries. Or sit there just after getting off of ferries, establishing their bearings. And yes as I write I know, I know that this may not always be so. Rumours and scuttlebutt reach me in my exile, and tell me that the Dún Laoghaire ferries are on their last legs. That *Ryanair* has done for them. That a hundred and something years of history is going down the pan, flushing out through the harbour mouth. And soon no more the *mailer* (as my generation had it), the car ferries, or the HSS. All going round that u-bend of history, to oblivion. Oh but no matter, and moving right along. Right beneath those blue mosaic seats is where the chairoplanes were erected.

Chairoplanes?

A carousel, little seats on the end of chains which whirl around. Very common in fairgrounds, even to this day. Here in Italy they call them *seggiolini volanti,* which sounds nice. The Dún Laoghaire chairoplanes were a health and safety nightmare and there was a story, an urban myth no doubt, that once the chains had broken on a particular seat and the occupant had flown through the air and landed in the harbour. That occupant was always described as a girl. Our culture likes the victim to be a girl. One wonders why…some sacrificial thing? The virgin to the flames, all that? Because the gods are into all that stuff? Oh well…whatever. Definitely whatever. Whatever about all that, those chairoplanes were certainly very popular with teenage girls. I imagine they gave them a licence to squeal and scream. And of course the chairoplanes were also very popular with teenage boys, because they could lean against the barriers looking up the girls' dresses as they whirled overhead.

Those were simpler days.

I leaned against the barrier looking up the girls' dresses as they whirled overhead. My bicycle leaned against the barrier beside me. And I had one eye on that, one eye on the thighs of the girls. Maybe even one and a half eyes on the bike, the remainder on the girls. Fairgrounds were dangerous places. Dangerous in that a bicycle could walk, if that's an appropriate expression. Walk, and in no time at all be pedalling some gurrier home to the 'Noggin. And to be honest…no matter how attractive the thighs of squealing girls there was no point in losing a bike over such an interest.

Now let's face it, despite what is said by the sexist and the boor (you know who you are, we drink together), one girl is not the same as the other. I've always realised that. And on this occasion I had my (one spare) eye on one particular girl who wasn't the same as anyone else. And she was C. Not that I knew her name at the time. That still nameless C stood out from the others. Or, rather, *sat* out from the others. She wasn't screaming, just kind of smiled. And she had her dress gripped some way between her knees in a manner which maintained a pleasing modicum of modesty. A yellow dress. And she had a pony tail. A blonde pony tail, tied up with yellow ribbons which matched her dress. Kind of stylish really. Well…for the times that were in it. And she was alone. And I was alone. And the fairground music played and the fairy lights lit up the night. People moved from shadow to shadow, wraiths. And the fairy lights hid more than they showed. There's actually something sinister about fairgrounds, in truth, there's clowns in those shadows. Killer clowns, with unpleasant private lives. And *The Joker* from *Batman* is never that far away. Oh yes I know all that now about fairgrounds… but then? More important things were on the mind.

Was, in fact, this girl, alone?

I looked around (with my bicycle watching eye) to see if some guy was waiting for her. Some big aggressive guy waiting for her. Some big possessive aggressive guy waiting for her. But there didn't seem to be anyone appropriate in the vicinity. *Carpe diem*, I told myself. But not in Latin of course. My Oxford double first in Greats was still some years away.

The chairoplanes carousel had a sort of picket fence around it, and there was a gap in this fence, a little gated gap where customers would go in and out. I moved myself and bicycle in that direction. And the gatekeeper watched me, suspiciously. He knew the score. He knew that in the rush of people coming out from the carousel there'd be sneakey little bastards going in, going in without paying. Sneakey little bastards just like me. And so he watched me, and I watched him. He smoked a roll up cigarette. And I felt good about things, because I wasn't going to try sneak in, I was just waiting for a girl. I didn't quite know what I would say when she emerged. In those days I didn't have a repertoire of chat up lines. I didn't actually even have one chat up line. So when she emerged through the gate all I could come up with was "I was watching you."

And she said "yes, I know."

This response told me that, if not precisely sorted, I was more or less in the zone. Or at the very least on the perimeter of the zone. Her response had that sardonic subtext which women use to signal interest. Not that I had at that stage come to terms with phrases like sardonic subtext, I just knew by instinct that that was the hidden meaning. I knew that, and also knew now that she had a strong working class accent. And I was middleclass and in those days the classes were very much apart from each other in Dún Laoghaire. Which sentence, as it pops up on screen, strikes me as one of the more absurd of a long writing life. And believe you me there's some competition in that regard. The sentence is absurd because nothing at all has changed. Except that nowadays the classes are even more apart. Because? No fairgrounds to bring them together? Ah but fuck it anyway, I'm not going there. Sociology is the curse of the creative.

I asked the girl her name and she told me, C. A nice name, originally French, but of course she didn't pronounce it in anything like the French manner. She had a strong working class accent. In fact that accent was so strong that I thought she was taking the piss of me and my middleclass tones. And maybe she was. But I won't know now.

C lived in Eden Villas in Glasthule, or so she told me between the chairoplanes and the roll-a-penny tables. And she worked in a vegetable shop up in Georges Street near the hospital, information she added between the roll-a-penny tables and the bumpers.

"Do you want to go on the bumpers?" she asked.

"I haven't got a lock for the bike," I told her.

"You think someone would steal that thing?"

"That's a bloody good bike," I protested, protective of my machine.

"And someone might steal it," she grinned, "someone from Eden Villas or somewhere like that?"

That simple sentence which identified our apartness brought us together.

"Someone from anywhere would like this bike," I told her sternly. And she made an oh-get-him gesture with her lips.

"Ah come on for Jesus' sake," she said, " leave it there we'll keep an eye on it."

We went on the bumpers. The seat was very tight and her thigh squeezed against mine. But then I suppose that was the whole point of bumping cars. Well not the whole point, but a major factor. Though bumping was the central theme. In those days bumping cars were bumping cars. Nothing dodgem about them. They were there for serious aggression. So the real major essential point of bumping cars, apart from squashing up with girls, was to inflict as much whiplash and internal injuries as possible upon the occupants of other cars. C and I whizzed around avoiding this scene but then one particular car started attacking us, following us, bashing from odd angles. This went on and on.

"Do you know those guys? I asked.

"Yes, fuckers from the buildings," she said.

The buildings then, a gruesome slum in Glasthule, made Eden Villas look like Shrewsbury Road. Now of course it's some kind of Corpo-run retirement home for distressed gentry who didn't make proper provision for their declining years. Things change.

"Right fuckers," added C. And barely were the words out of her mouth when there was an almighty shunt from the rear. C lost it, turned round, stood half up in the car and shrieked "would you ever fuck off you bollixes." Well, that was her general drift. And then she sat down quietly beside me. And adjusted her dress about her knees demurely. Her hands were very pretty.

"You know, C," I said, "when I was watching you on the chairoplanes I said to myself that's a nice quiet girl."

"I am a nice quiet girl" she said.

She was.

We left the funfair and walked quietly along the seafront. Somewhere near the King George Monument I held her hand. She knitted her fingers into mine. We walked on. Past the Baths and somewhere opposite Teddy's we had a snog. We walked on. We looked at the sea. It was one of those nights. The rippley black water like sheets of that wrapping paper they put round precious things in exclusive shops. I know that now but didn't then. All I knew then was the quietness of the sea and C beside me. And I reckon that was enough. She told me that she often came down here from Eden Villas to look at the sea. And I told her she was lucky, living so near to it. And she laughed. I suppose because by then I'd told her I lived in Killiney. And she reckoned I didn't know I was born, luck-wise.

We walked on.

On along Newtownsmith and up Islington Avenue. Another snog

there in a lane, my hand up her blouse on her breasts. We crossed Summerhill Road near the church. I had made my Holy Communion there. It seemed a long while ago. It seems even longer now as I write.

We walked into Eden Park and along the terrace opposite the church. In those days there was a little alleyway at the end of terrace, going up between the wall of Pres and the high gables of the houses. That alleyway is still there but it was different then, the first part just being a narrow path between dense shrubberies on each side. Oh yes it's very different now, all that the greenery cleared away to make a wide path, almost a roadway. No doubt this done to give access to the mews at the back and also to cut back on antisocial activities. Or indeed, cut back on the very social activities which C and I were headed for.

We ducked into the shrubberies. She watched me manoevering the bike through the bushes.

"Would you ever leave that bloody bike down" she said.

"I can't leave it out on the path. Told you I had no lock."

"Jesus Christ Almighty" she said.

We made love in the bushes. We were very young so I suppose that expression would better be typed as *we had sex in the bushes*. But that sounds cold, and it wasn't cold, we seemed to be very fond of each other. And best now to keep old memories warm. There's coldness enough in the grave ahead. Women are lovely, I realised, watching her settle her clothes back together. Lovely, and practical too. That I knew, with a suddenness. And the years since have added a few more words to the understanding.

Once out of the bushes we walked on, my arm on her shoulder and my other hand pushing the bike. I'd unwrapped her hair from the ponytail, the better to play with it round her face, and it fell now on my arm like a veil. Yes, like a veil, exactly what I thought then, like a veil. Like one of those veils on one of those little girls who had made their Holy Communion with me back there in the church. I actually glanced behind at the church. As if looking into time. But I didn't see into time. Just saw stone. And it looked pretty damn grim, and dark. Grim and dark and cold in the way of the stone of churches.

We walked on, across the Lower Eden Road. Then up past Eden Terrace. Past Findlater Street. Past Coldwell Street and into the villas. Eden Villas. Indian territory to me from Killiney. She stopped at a particular gate.

"What now?" I said.

She shook her head, and shrugged.

I kissed her on the forehead. Played with her hair some more. And got on the bike and cycled away. Past Coldwell Street. Findlater Street. Eden Terrace. Then along into Hudson Road and up Albert Road. And at the top of Albert Road in those days there was a crossroads, not a roundabout. It's changed a lot, but the hill hasn't. I got off the bike there and walked. Up Killiney Road. Thoughtful.

Yes of course we met again.

But I left Ireland soon after. England, Sweden, Spain. Lots of countries, and lots of other girls. Some of their names I remember, some not. But I always remember C. I suppose one does. And then after many years I met her again. Decades. She was still working in a vegetable shop up in DúnLaoghaire. And I was buying carrots. And her hair was short now. But still blonde. With help from Peter Mark.

"You should always buy vegetables in a vegetable shop," she told me. "Much fresher than a supermarket."

"I always do," I said, watching her place carrots on the weighing machine. Her hands were very pretty. I remembered her adjusting her dress in that bumping car of long ago. And I suppose she did too. I remembered her putting her breasts back into her bra in the Glasthule shrubberies. And I suppose she did too.

"Good," she said, "support the independent retailer."

"I do my best," I assured, and then asked her was she still living in Eden Villas. She shook her head.

"We got a house in Ballybrack. You still have that bike?"

My turn to shake my head.

"Flash car I suppose," she grinned.

"Not particularly."

She looked at me, carefully. And turned away. And spoke to the carrots as she put them in a plastic bag. "It was a long time ago, wasn't it?"

"Thirty years" I said.

"And the rest."

She gave me the carrots. I gave her the money. And her hands were very very pretty, her wedding ring a circle round a life I did not know. It closed me out, defended. But I did not really want to know anyway. Because if I did I'd want her different colours in her paintbox. And time and it's tanglings are not mine to unravel. Best leave that to Dr Hawking, Dr Who.

Time and its…Jeez…that meeting itself was ten years ago, probably more. And I never saw her again. And whether she be alive or dead I have no idea. A Granny in Ballybrack? Or a name down in Shanganagh on a stone? *Beloved Wife. And Mum. And Nan.*

But whoever…and whatever…and wherever…she's a ghost. But a particular ghost. Like a face on a passing bus that you know among the strangers. A particular ghost who shares much more than a name with that other ghost in Nottingam Road…in that creaky old hotel in Kwazulu Natal.

Outside that grave I know so well.

Their haunting is the one.

I reckon that ghost is my gatekeeper, between my past and my future.

Between my secrets, and my stories.

C.

Raleigh...Vespa...Honda

THE GIRLS WERE SITTING in a circle in the dust, each one doing another's hair. And each one simultaneously having her own hair done by the one alongside. But they stopped at this when they saw me arrive, and giggled among themselves. I ignored them, parked the bike. No, not the teenager's Raleigh bike, a big motorbike this time. Honda. Nice machine. And why not, I was in my twenties and important. I had come about the well. I had come to the village to talk to the infumu, the man. I wasn't going to get into banter with a gaggle of village girls doing mukule. A gaggle of traditional tribal girls in a remote village in central Africa. A gaggle of traditional bare breasted tribal girls. To be avoided, that lot. Bare breasts are best come in twos, any more than that tend to be intimidating.

I ignored them, and walked importantly past. I was important. I had a gun in case people tried to kill me. But fat lot of good that did me now. Here my only defence against the giggling of these teenage girls was stoicism. Stiff upper lip. White man's burden sort of stuff. And the dignity of that roll of drawings under my arm something akin to that fasces, that bundle of sticks wrapped round an axe that was carried by Roman Empire functionaries. Symbol of authority. My drawings marked me out. As important.

Pity though. Because also, to the girls, they marked me out as ridiculous.

Dead right they were too. Because your white man in Africa is, of course, ridiculous. Be he soldier or missionary, aid worker or technician, he is essentially a clown. And all his works mere jokes, routines. His Africa has the reality of a circus tent, a theatre, a music hall, a palace of variety. And when the white man leaves the stage the roof falls in. That's just the way of it.

But a man goes to Africa because a man goes to Africa. And I suppose he's a particular sort of guy that goes on that journey. Maybe it's the blackness in him. Nothing mystical, no, just something physical in the actual dna. Maybe even though he's white he does have some racial inheritance, some hidden strand of genes that tick along and just have to go back home. Yes best to go home to Africa in those circumstances. Or perhaps there is actually something mystical, and it's a different sort of blackness draws him there, a darkness. A shadow on the soul. Because that is one dark place. But there again…it's also blindingly bright, and friendly and funny as well, in short it's very human. And very what we humans are. All in all it's not surprising that we come from there, and something calls us back. And I went there from a jail in Wicklow.

Literally. And not literally in the sense of *it was literally raining cats and dogs*. No, in the sense of reality. I did in reality go there from a jail. Yes ok the jail was spelt *gaol* for some archaic reason, but I was still confined to a cell… in Wicklow *Gaol*. My employers Wicklow County Council called it an office, but that didn't fool me. The place had bars on the windows and a heavy door with a spyhole. I had gone to UCD school of architecture and it hadn't taught me much. But I did know a jail/gaol cell when I was cooped up in one.

The Raleigh bike had been sold when I was seventeen and I'd gone travelling and come back and gone to college and my wheels were now a

Vespa. And I was working as an assistant in the engineering department of Wicklow County Council. Essentially I was in charge of my boss's nixers, spending most of my day doing drawings for his private clients. People extending pubs and bungalows and applying for planning permission...from himself. To say that Wicklow County Council was corrupt in those days is an understatement. Like saying well actually it's quite difficult to get to the moon. But that's the Irish public service for you, its role to serve that part of the public who are bureaucrats. It's an Irish thing. Something to do with Cromwell and a difficult history fraught.

But not to exaggerate, I did actually do some work on behalf of the County Council itself, and this is where the Vespa came in. Living in Dún Laoghaire I had to ride some distance to get to work. Some distance to even get as far as the Wicklow border at Bray. And Bray is not really Wicklow, being some kind of independent satrap, much like Monaco is to France. Perhaps not as attractive as a physical location, but nonetheless it does have certain Monaco similarities. It's by the sea and there are gambling facilities. And it's controlled by a cabal of hereditary town councillors on behalf of the overlords. In Monaco's case these overlords are in Paris, and in that of Bray in Wicklow Town. Same difference really. Although Paris does not pretend to be Wicklow Town.

It's a hell of a long way away on a Vespa, Wicklow Town. And it was even further in those days, the roads not up to their current scratch. But mercifully I didn't have to go there every day, and sometimes not even every week. That cell in the old *Gaol* was merely Basecamp One. My real job was to travel round North County Wicklow surveying council houses. The tenantry had recently been given the opportunity to buy these from the Council, and there was a necessity to prepare drawings and maps and so forth for the legalities. My job also involved some kind of census, in that the Council had more or less forgotten which houses they owned and which they didn't. And in fact the very existence of some was a mystery. There were places on tops of mountains that essentially no longer existed in records. Places that a rent collector only got to every twenty years. And of course rent collectors die, and institutional memory gets lost. And such were the days before computerisation.

All very interesting. And I met lots of interesting housewives. Many of them slatterns who made sexual advances. Like cartoon housewives in milkman jokes. Wicklow produces slatterns like North County Dublin produces vegetables. It's the thing there. Perhaps something to do with the mountains, allied to the frontier mentality. Places on the borders of very big cities are like that, must be that. Someone in the ESRI probably knows the answer. Anyway all in all Wicklow is and was primitive and earthy and I was young and very good looking. And I did have a clipboard and a measuring tape, which marked me out, not to mention a Vespa. So all in all it was a good job, but could nonetheless be difficult. I remember a woman in Killincarrig who's house and garden were so complex in their layout that I had to go back week after week to finalise their details. Week after week. It was great. She had red hair and a husband on the bins.

But there's a downside to being a young man on a Vespa in County Wicklow. This has mostly got to do with rain. It rained a lot. And while it is quite possible to stay reasonably dry on a Vespa scooter, that possibility does diminish after miles and miles of Wicklow mountain. And it's not the only thing that diminishes. The lights go out in the spirit, one by one. And the soul gets down to a glimmer. And that glimmer does little to brighten a jail cell basecamp one. Oops, sorry, *gaol* cell basecamp one.

I jacked it in. They didn't give me a farewell party. But that's Wicklow for you. Wicklow women will give you a shag quicker than a kind word, and Wicklow men...well, to understand them just go to a GAA match in Donard or round those parts. Bring a riot shield. They're tribal.

I jacked it in and rode the Vespa for the last time from Wicklow Town back to Dún Laoghaire. It was a thoughtful journey, a cusp, a watershed. And my thoughts went back, and forth. The houses I designed in Laragh Village, and their steep pitched alpine roofs. The redhead in Killincarrig. An absolute slattern but I've always loved slatterns, their reality. And I'm more than a bit of a one myself. I thought of such things, and how all of life was farce and drama.

It was around Kilmacanogue that I saw him, a boy on a bicycle, riding a brand new Raleigh bicycle in the Dublin direction. I slowed down on the Vespa and followed him, thoughtfully. He pedalled on, determined. That is one tough kid, I decided, he'll go far.

I followed the boy all the way to Shankill, and watched as he stopped at a bench there. And watched as he got off the bike and sat beside a man who had been waiting there, waiting for him. And I saw the man's car parked slightly up the road a bit, carefully away from the busstop. A Morris Oxford car. How old fashioned it looked. And the boy's clothes, and the man's too, how old fashioned they seemed as well.

I waited in the background as they talked. The man was finishing a cigarette, and the smoke drifted. In the memory now a dance of wraiths in blue. He stood up then and stamped his cigarette out. With the twist of a heel that you knew was his particular habit, and had some meaning. And then he walked to his car and drove away. Walked to that old fashioned car in his old fashioned suit. And drove away.

The boy got back on the bike and cycled on. I followed him to Shankill where he paused, deciding. Deciding to go over the hill or around on the flatter way. I knew which way he'd go. And I almost told him no, take the easier. But the telling wasn't mine to tell. He headed up the hill and I passed him there, accelerating. He was struggling against it. And I was his future, leading him. I glanced back every now and then to see how he was going, and there he was, struggling, but determined. And then one time I glanced back and he was no longer there. And I reckoned we had merged into the one again. And our spinning wheels were all the one.

Raleigh, Vespa…and then Honda.

Yes, I went to Africa and there I rode my Honda motorbike to places dangerous and tranquil, sometimes both. The job was all about wells, and roads and drains. And putting tin roofs where once was thatch. Development, yeah right, good word. I designed little houses and supervised their building. And sometimes wonder now just what remains. What remains of my little IBR roofed concrete houses? IBR?

Inverted Broad Ridge, a type of corrugated sheeting. Something similar is used in Ireland, *Agribuild*. Used for agricultural buildings, for barns and housing animals, that sort of usage. Do the math.

I was very proud of my little African houses, and often worry about their fate. Are they bullet riddled, abandoned, scorched by fire? What remains of them? And what remains of the teenage girls? They who had giggled at me because I was ridiculous, what of them? And the question answers itself, that rape is a weapon in war. And these are dangerous times, there's lots of wars. The world is in an unravelling, and a rage.

I ask myself again. What remains of my little African houses? And what remains of those pretty girls? And asking myself those questions I remember what I know, and what I know is that questions tend to hide, each behind another. Like those twin stars only found by modern science, but always known to myth. All questions are shadows of another, and the one that casts the shadow is always a bigger question. And so my questions about Africa are really asking...boy on a bicycle, young man on a motorbike...what remains of him?

Everything, I reckon...and the because?

The spinning wheels are all the one.

A Different Bike

YES, I HAD BEEN SEVENTEEN when I sold the bicycle of those younger teenage years. I cycled it into Dublin and sold it in a secondhand bike shop. I'm sure I was robbed but it gave me enough. And I used the money to buy a ticket to London on the mailboat. The first leg of a journey that brought me to Europe, and Africa. And then back again to Europe. And in those seven or eight years I never rode a bicycle.

But you never forget, or so they say. And on a certain day in a certain year I was in Amsterdam. I was travelling with my South African girl, Leone. And we'd met a Dutch couple who were putting us up in their apartment. For the generosity, and I reckon because we were interesting. It doesn't take that much to be interesting among Dutch people. And one day they lent us bicycles, their personal bicycles. And Leone and I rode out of the city, way out into the flat countryside. It was cyclists' heaven.

We stopped by a canal and watched barges. And yes, there was a windmill. And yes, as well, there was one of those strange tilting bridges that Van Gogh might have painted. And probably did. We sat on the grass there, the bicycles beside us, one upon the other. I don't know why we put the bicycles like that. It's not sensible really. The pedals or handlebars of one always seem to get wrapped with the other. It's like waking up with a woman. There's always a stray arm or leg in some kind of entanglement. Nature's way, I reckon.

I sat beside Leone, and she was thoughtful, quiet. And so I got up and wandered around, mooching. And looked back at her and she was ever so beautiful. She really was, honestly, beautiful, blonde, Afrikaans. And with the faintest touch of some darker race in there, unmentioned, maybe even unmentionable, a message from some ancestral liaison. How much do I love thee, I thought, and other expressions like that, poetical. Me Byron, you reader! I watched her and the breeze stirred her hair. And she reached up and settled it. But kept her fingers there, twiddling, and thinking.

I looked at the barge passing. And a man waved. No, not waved, raised the flat of his hand in some salute. I suppose he was saluting the beautiful Leone, and not me. Damn sure he was, she was a bargeman's dream. And I saw her smile, and how she let go her hair and opened the fingers of her hand in acknowledgement. I noticed the bargeman's hat, it was so familiar, like he had to dress for the part. And then I watched the windmill, but the vanes were still and I wondered why, because there was a breeze. There had to be a breeze, I told myself, because Leone's hair was drifting in it. And why weren't the vanes...oh to hell with it...I decided I just didn't know that much about windmills.

I looked at the bicycles. And remembered being that boy on the bicycle in Dún Laoghaire. Not the details, nor anything of those stories I've written here in these pages. No, just the memory. And then the ripples of the memory like the wake of that barge gone by on the canal. We untangled the bicycles and cycled back into the city. Gave them back to their owners and travelled on. Through Germany and Denmark and Sweden. And those months were the years of our togetherness. Then way up there in the snow we had a falling out, Leone and I. And she went to Finland and I to Spain. Yes, that's a falling out. The long distance variety. We never saw each other again. But stayed in touch. And thirty years later she wrote to me from South Africa and told me she had cancer. By way of saying goodbye, I reckoned. Such a message hardly says hello.

My cycling days were long done. As were my Vespa scooter days, not to mention the Honda motorbike. I was now a four wheeled guy, the extra wheels some compensation for the thinning hair, something along those lines. But I did have another temporary sort of bicycle at the exact time that I heard from Leone in KwaZulu Natal. A Peugeot this time, expensive, no nonsense. I'd been ill myself, and had bought it for the health, recovering. I was back living in Dún Laoghaire. In another life, with beloved wife, and children. Happy with the wife, and children. But unhappy with a woman lost, a child lost, and children unborn, and lives not lived. Unhappy, but still I knew…if a man doesn't have that unhappiness he hasn't lived himself. I took out the fancy Peugeot bike and cycled off, around Glenageary. I thought of Leone, dying, far away. And I thought of our bicycles, entangled on a canal path, far away. And my bike wrapped with hers like bodies on a sleepy morning.

Different bike, same boy.

I cycled down the Metals, because it's a good place to be alone. And it's a place where a guy can get up a fair old speed on a fancy Peugeot racing bike. I whizzed along. And I thought of Leone, and what she had meant to me, back then. And soon the redness of the red African earth around her bones. *Oh koud is die windjie*, I thought, remembering a poem she had taught me in her own harsh language. *Oh koud is die windjie*. Cold is the breeze. I thought of that. And I thought of all the ways of life and love and loss. And yes, I thought of that other bike, the clunkey Raleigh that I had back in my teens.

Different bike.

Same boy.

Extracts from Conan Kennedy's latest fiction start on following page.

They say....

On the face of it, Kennedy writes straightforward detective stories, but with his slow burning plots, his complexity unfolds page by page, drawing the reader in to a world of beguiling mystery.

www.acommonreader.org

Conan Kennedy paints his characters so thoroughly you can feel their breath on your face. The fact that the author is also a poet oozes from his writing like wine from a press. His staccato dialogue, spoken and narrated, and his techniques borrowed more from the song of poetry than the grammar of prose, weave a compelling texture of emotion, description and story telling.

www.acclaimedbooks.com

An extract from
Conan Kennedy's

The Colour
of Her
Eyes

Prologue

Mum and Dad brought him to Bognor in the summer. Not every weekend, but maybe once or twice a month. He was five, or six. They lived in Horsham then. Dad worked in a shoeshop. They didn't have a car, but got one later when Dad became a manager, in a shoeshop.

They went to Bognor on the bus. It was so exciting. Those buses were green and cream, Southdown Motor Company. The number sixty nine, that was the bus, Horsham to Bognor. It was quite a long journey really. Horsham to Pulborough and through Petworth and Midhurst, places like that. And Arundel. Mum always pointed out the castle there. Then they went through Ford. Dad always pointed out the prison. And said that's where you'll end up, if you're a bold boy. And Mum said don't pay any attention to your Dad, he's only joking.

It was quite a long journey, but worth every minute. They had such a good time in Bognor. It was disappointing when they didn't go. Some summer weekends they just stayed at home in Horsham. Or maybe went off somewhere else, for a trip. And sometimes on those weekends he saw a Southdown bus on the streets. There weren't that many. Most of the buses around Horsham in those days were from other companies, and there were London buses too. But when he saw the green and cream Southdown bus, the number sixty nine, and when they weren't going away on it, he got quite upset. And Mum would say, we'll go next week.

Sometimes they did, go next week, sometimes they didn't. But when they did it was always the same, always exciting. Which was strange, that it was exciting, because they always did the same things. One weekend was much the same as the next. They would

112

walk through the town from the bus station. That was in the High Street then. It's gone now. Down past the bowling green, where Dad would always say to Mum well we must give that a try some day. And she would laugh, but the child didn't know why, and she'd say I'll wait until I'm a little older. And Mum and Dad would laugh together, and he would put his arm around her shoulder.

They'd walk down the pier, and Mum would say stay away from the edge, John. And Dad would read rude postcards at the stalls. And he'd show some of them to Mum, and they'd both laugh together, and look at each other, something mysterious in their faces. They were very young then. He was the only child, and they didn't have much money. They never had any more children. After the pier they'd walk along the esplanade, towards Felpham. And they always stopped at a particular place. Mum called it our place. They'd sit in deckchairs and a man would come along with a ticket machine to collect money. And Mum would have brought sandwiches, and biscuits. And in those days you could buy a pot of tea at stalls.

He'd play on the beach. There was always other children, and they all played together. And sometimes Dad would stroll down to the edge of the water, and throw stones into the sea. And he would run over to him, and throw stones too. And Dad showed him how to skim stones, so they'd hop across the water. But he wasn't really strong enough for that. He was only five, or six or seven. So he just had to content himself with throwing stones out onto the water, and watching the ripples that they made. And then that was it, more or less. They'd pack up their things, and walk back to the bus station. Past the pier and past the crazy golf and past the bowling green. The players there looked like snowmen to him, in their whites, ghostly snowmen in the gloom of the evening, moving slowly.

Back at the bus station they'd get on the bus. Green and cream, Southdown Motor Services. Back to Horsham, through Midhurst, Petworth, and places like that. It was sometimes quite dark when they got home. He'd lie in bed, listening to Mum and Dad, making love in the next room. He didn't know they were making love, too young to know. He just knew that they sounded happy. Mum was giggling. And as he listened he'd see in his mind the sea at Bognor. And the ripples from the stones he had thrown into the water. And he'd think of the ripples, going far away forever. To Australia even.

Mum never got old enough to play bowls in Bognor. She died at thirty two. Pulmonary embolism. It was very sudden. Life changed a lot, then, in Horsham. They never went to Bognor anymore. It wouldn't have been the same. He grew up. He went to Sussex University and then teacher training college in London. From there one particular saturday he went to Victoria Station, and took the train to Bognor. Just for the afternoon. On the journey he saw that station sign for Ford. And remembered Dad saying to him he'd end up there if he was a bold boy. Ford Prison. He didn't see Arundel Castle, maybe he was on the wrong side of the train. When he got to Bognor he walked from the station down to the esplanade. Past the bowling green where Mum never got to play. And then down onto the beach. He walked along to the place that Mum used call our place. And he sat in a deckchair there, watching.

When he got bored with watching he went down to the shoreline and threw stones. And watched the ripples on the water. He imagined Mum and Dad sitting up there in deckchairs, watching him. But when he looked around there was just empty deckchairs flapping in the breeze. Mum was dead and Dad was too, by then. He'd never really been the same. Alcoholism.

He walked back to the station. It was early for the train. He went into the pub there in Station Road. There was a bunch of guys and girls there that he knew. He'd known them at Sussex University. They were going back to London. And there was other students with them that he didn't know. They all went back together to London. On the train he found himself sitting beside a Belgian girl, one of the students he hadn't known before. She was very pretty. Her name was Yvette De Donnea. He married her.

One

SUSSEX POLICE. ARUN DISTRICT. BOGNOR SOUTH.
TRANSCRIPT.
11.15. 20 March
DI HARRIS - John Stanley Dexter

"Yes, she was a pretty girl, if I remember rightly."

"What does that mean, if you remember? She was either pretty, or she wasn't."

"It's an expression."

"I don't need expressions. I need to know. Anyway, it doesn't strike me as being an expression. Strikes me as being an evasion."

"You reckon?"

"Yeah I reckon. Strikes me as you saying you don't really want to admit she was pretty. Or that you found her pretty."

"Why would I do that?"

"Hey. We have a system here. It goes like this. I ask a question. You answer."

"Ask away."

"So, you tell me, why would you not want to admit? That she was pretty?"

"I don't know...why I would do that. There's no reason."

"There's a reason for everything."

"I disagree."

"I know you do, you believe in chance. Or let's put it this way, you say you believe in chance. Coincidences."

"I prefer to call them correspondences. Parallel sort of things, happening."

"Call them what you fucking well like. I'm not going into that psychic *crap. Just answer the fucking question. Was she pretty?"*

"I suppose so."

"You suppose? If you remember rightly?"

"OK, she was pretty."

"She was pretty. Jesus how long is this going to take."

"Takes as long as it takes, I suppose."

"I wasn't asking you. It was just..."

"An expression?"

"Don't fuck around with me John. What was she wearing?"

"When?"

"What do you mean when, when when when, what are we talking about here?"

"A dance. A school dance. A disco. She was wearing what you'd wear at a dance."

"I wouldn't wear what she was wearing. I'm not a fourteen year old girl."

"You're kidding? You had me there for a minute."

"What was she wearing?"

"I told you, she was wearing what a girl would wear, dancing, clubbing."

"You didn't, you told me she was wearing what I, me, a Sussex copper, what I would wear at a dance."

"I meant what one would wear at a dance. One."

"Enough of the fucking English grammar lesson, you're not a schoolteacher. Anymore."

"Once a teacher, always a teacher."

"Once a fucking evasive bastard, always a fucking evasive bastard. Look John, the point is. The reason we're sitting here. You were a schoolteacher then, at that disco. So, tell me, what was she wearing?"

"A skirt."

"No top? Like some kind of south sea maiden?"

"Of course she was wearing a top. I just started by mentioning the skirt."

"Why?"

"Probably because they usually wear jeans."

"Who, who usually wear jeans?"

"Girls, teenagers."

"You spend a lot of time looking at teenage girls?"

"I was a teacher, didn't have much choice."

"I didn't say spent, I said spend. The present tense. I said you spend a lot of time looking at teenage girls. It was a question."

"No more than most, men, I suppose."

"So you're just an average sort of creep, rather than a special one. Jesus. Anyway. This skirt. What sort of skirt?"

"What do you mean?"

"Like was it a dress kind of skirt, sort of flowing skirt, to the ankles, or a little short job?"

"Short."

"Why didn't you say that? Why didn't you say she was wearing a short skirt?"

"I hadn't got to the detail."

"Yeah, right. This whole conversation has the same problem. Nice legs?"

"Nice legs?"

"Yes, that's what I said, that's what I asked. I'll ask again. Did the girl, the pretty girl, the pretty fourteen year old girl, did she have nice legs?"

"Unusual."

"What do you mean? Like she'd no knees or something?"

"Unusual just to have legs, or to see legs, because ordinarily these kids would wear jeans."

"So the legs came as a surprise?"

"You could put it like that."

"I am putting it like that. You're telling me...let's get this precise...you didn't expect this girl to have legs. So what the fuck do you think they all have under their jeans? Sticks?"

117

"It was just a bit of a shock."

"Good legs, huh? Nice thighs? You a leg or a tit man?"

"I don't know, really."

"I think you're a leg man."

"What makes you so sure?"

"Because you didn't mention her top. The top she was wearing."

"I hadn't got round to that."

"It's where you start that counts. I know what she was wearing on top."

"Do you? How?"

"Two reasons really. One I'm a detective inspector of police, I know what's going on. In society. With teenagers. All that."

"And the other reason?"

"I'm a tit man. And I'm telling you she was wearing a skimpy little top with her tits poking out one end and her belly the other. Am I right?"

"Not quite."

"Where did I go wrong?"

"Well in those days you wouldn't see their stomach. It wasn't the fashion."

"OK, you're the expert. On underage girls. I'm only the amateur here. But I bet I'm half right. I bet her tits were falling out of the top."

"It was pretty low cut, yes."

"You in the fashion business, the rag trade?"

"You know I'm not."

"Well stop saying things like it was pretty low cut. What we both mean is her fucking tits were falling out of her fucking top. Am I right?"

"OK, you're right."

"Good. Now. So what do we have here. This little teenage poppet. Tits all over the shop. With nice thighs."

"I didn't say that. Didn't say anything about thighs."

"No you didn't, but you said she was wearing a skirt."

"That is not the same thing."

"Did she not have nice thighs?"

"Well I suppose all young girls have nice thighs."

"Do you? Do you suppose that?"

"Well you know what I mean."

"No I don't. Don't tell me I know what you mean. Tell me what you mean. Hey, by the way, what colour were her eyes?

"Green."

"So you remember that, immediately. Kind of vague about her legs, her tits, but you remember her eyes. Now why is that?"

"You tell me."

"I'm going to think about that John, think about it."

*

The green eyed girl came over to help.

Or did she, John Dexter wondered, did she really come to help?

Was that the reason he found her, standing there, hovering about?

Or was that just an accident, an accident of timing, of when she came and when he came?

Was she in fact part of the group, the gang that had caused the damage?

Could be. That bunch had scattered pretty sharpish, seeing him coming. Disappeared into the mob of dancers. And did this girl just happen to be left behind? Was she someone who hadn't been quite quick enough to merge back into the crowd?

Suspicions, thinking like that. Yep, he admitted it to himself, it's happened. Happened already. I'm asking myself those questions, suspicious questions. Six months teaching and already he hated the little fuckers. Oh ok, put it a bit more diplomatically, he just didn't trust teenagers.

Because he was close enough to them in age? Only about five or six years since he'd been one himself. Yes maybe that was the reason, the reason he didn't trust them. But whatever. The reasons weren't important. The facts were. Here in the school now he felt geriatric. And only six months in, if that. Six months in to a career. What a word, career. Something death row about the sound of it.

John Dexter sighed, and sighed. Grim view of the world, dim view of the pupils. God knows what his opinion would be by retirement.

Retirement?

Another bad word. It sort of rhymed with pension. And mortgage. Not to mention disappointment.

"Ok, ok, ok. We better get this cleaned up," he said to her, looking at the rubble on the floor.

"What a mess," she said.

"What's your name?"

"Moonshine," she replied.

"Your name is not Moonshine," he said, dropping a tired pause into the spaces between each word. And I don't care what the name is, he thought, he just felt tired. Extremely tired. And tiredly he started kicking bits of the rubble into a heap with the side of his foot.

She looked at him. "Your name is Mr Dexter, innit?"

"How do you know?"

"Some of the girls fancy you."

"Well, that's nice. Better that than some of the boys," he added. Though, looking around at some of the girls, he wondered.

She laughed, but not much. And then she started kicking at the stuff from the other direction. He watched her feet, down there in those high heeled sandals. Nice feet, he thought. If this was a dream I could kiss her feet and lick her toes. But this was Walthamstow. And this was not a dream.

They don't do dreams in Walthamstow. But there again, she had a nice laugh. OK she looked rough, very rough. But then, why shouldn't rough looking girls have nice laughs? No reason. And why the hell shouldn't they have nice feet? Very nice feet. Her toenails were varnished scarlet. And was that a real tattoo on her ankle, or one of those stick on efforts?

No matter.

I am not going to kiss her feet and lick her toes, he realised. Because the more he looked at her, the more she seemed to be very young. And the older he felt. And the less interested. And even her real name, he couldn't be arsed, he just couldn't be bothered. He was tired. It was late. He was too fucking old to be at a teenagers' disco. But it was work. A teacher's work. Mr Girdlestone the Head had laid it on the line.

"Important to bond with the young people, John."

"I completely agree," Dexter had said.

Little choice. A few months into the job and his role was to completely agree. But bond? Bond my arse he thought, there was no bonding with this lot. They were different. Probably mutants. Brain dead from computer games. And those food additives in ready meals, none of that could have helped. Bond? Yeah right. Not hard to notice that Mr Girdlestone himself was not in the hall, no sign of him bonding with the young people. No chance. Hiding in his office, no doubt. Notorious for hiding in his office, Mr Girdlestone spent his days writing poetry, or so the teachers laughed. Very bad poetry. A very bad poet, at the head of a very bad school.

Bloody Walthamstow, Dexter thought, bloody Walthamstow. And this bloody girl. What the hell did it matter what her name was? Nothing. He shrugged. No point in arguing the toss. Let her be Moonshine. Snowflake. Marge Simpson. It didn't matter. He didn't have to know. He'd never even seen her before. And might not ever again. She definitely wasn't in any of his classes, would have remembered her. And if he did ever need to know her real name, he'd find out. Right now there was more immediate things. Suddenly he saw his thinking glinting in some mirror of the mind. And that made him grin to himself. Like there was a joke going around.

"What you grinning at?" the girl said.

"Nothing, nothing," he said quickly, stopping grinning. No it wasn't that amusing. And it was terrible really how a teacher gets into this frame of mind so damn quickly. So bloody negative. Come to work. Do what's now. Try to keep a lid on most stuff. Go home.

"You're mocking me, taking the piss, that grin."

"I am not," and he was nearly going to add "do you know what the word paranoid means," but she wouldn't, she wouldn't know. So he held his peace, and just continued sliding the rubble into a pile with the side of his foot, watching his shoe, and how it was getting dirty, dusty.

Those were his black leather shoes, his only black leather shoes. And, in fact, the only pair of black leather shoes on a male in this entire school hall. Oh yes, he'd noticed that, earlier. The kids wore canvas trainers, or plastic or whatever they were. With logos. And the other male teachers on duty had dressed down to that standard. Yes he knew that older men teachers tend to do that, as if deliberately setting out to look ridiculous. But even Karl Evans over there, the same age as himself, even he was dressed like one of the pupils. Not that that surprised him.. Dexter had been to College with Karl Evans, and knew that he had an instinct for these things. Tended to fit in, automatically. Maybe next disco he himself would do the same, wear trainers. Now that he knew the form. Best always to feel one's way into these things. Err on the side of caution.

John Dexter was a fairly cautious sort of person.

He kicked at the mess. It wasn't really rubble on the floor, couldn't be described as that. It was just the remains of a large ceramic plant pot which had toppled from its stand. Or, perhaps more precisely, a pot which had been toppled...yes, had, been, toppled, from its stand. It now lay smashed, and scattered in a spill of earth or compost across the floor. The plant itself lay there too, its roots freed from the soil. Reminded him somehow of a dead fish, washed up out of its element.

"What we need is a brush," he said to the girl, "a brush and pan."

No, he didn't say, he shouted at the girl. The noise was horrendous.

"Pan?" she looked at him.

That's when he really noticed the green eyes.

What extraordinary eyes, he thought. But then he thought of something else, something awful. God, this girl doesn't know what a pan is. It's meltdown. Social collapse. In another generation they won't know what a brush is for.

"The thing that goes with the brush," he explained, astonished, "for sweeping up. Little flat thing."

"Oh yeah," she said, "Gran has one of them."

Good for Gran, he thought. "Tell you what," he said, "there'll be brushes and so on in the cleaners' cupboard in the corridor. Would you go like a good girl and get them."

"I'll go," she said, and paused. "Like a good girl."

That's when he noticed her grin.

"And get a bucket, to put all this stuff into." He kicked the rubble together a little more, as if to demonstrate what he needed the bucket for. "I'll stay here and stop kids kicking it all over the place."

"As if they would," she said, and left.

He watched her, going. Skinny? No. Not skinny. Slender was the more appropriate word. A skinny young girl becomes slender. It's a tipping point, that. One day skinny, next day slender. Go to bed skinny, wake up slender. Mysterious. But not half as mysterious as how do they walk on those ridiculous high heels? And is she deliberately waggling her arse like that? Do they make a decision to waggle their arse? Or is it just nature's mysterious way, like going to bed skinny and waking up slender?

Oh Christ, what the fuck does it matter.

Wondering and thinking about all this stuff achieves nothing, Dexter decided. Except to mark me out as even more of an old fogey. He turned away from watching and just stood there, guarding his pile of rubble in its little heap. Wished he was at home, really. Or down the pub.The launderette? Even.

The noise here was, yes, horrendous. In strict legal terms, he imagined, teachers on supervision duty should have been issued with ear muffs, like blokes on building sites operating pneumatic drills. The noise here was just as bad. Alright for the kids, they were immune to it anyway, half deaf already from music wired into their ears, but it was definitely a threat to teachers' health. Twenty years time and my hearing is shot, well then someone will be hearing from my solicitors.

Twenty years time. He sighed, picking the words out of the thought.

Twenty years of this?

The return of the green eyed girl put a stop to that line of thought.

Yes, she had found a brush, and a bucket, and a pan, even if she didn't quite know the purpose of the last item. He showed her how, how it worked, and it was like demonstrating some amazing new piece of technology. Between them order was restored to their little spot of floor. The bucket was full.

"What will I do with the plant," he wondered aloud, holding it and looking at her.

Something in her eyes made him immediately sorry he had spoken. He waited for it. It came.

"You could stick it up the headmaster's arse," she said.

"Now," he raised a schoolteachery hand, he paused. Then added, "let's have none of that."

"Now Moonshine," she said.

"I beg your pardon?"

"You said now, to give out to me, and then you were going to say my name, but you hesitated, 'cos you didn't know it. So you just did without it."

She was right.

"Very observant of you."

"Moonshine," she corrected.

"Sorry?"

"Very observant of you, Moonshine, that's what you should say."

"I'm not going to get involved in that nonsense. If you want to tell me your real name you will, if you don't, please yourself. Why don't you get back to your friends, to the dance...or whatever that jumping around is...I'll look after the bucket."

"And the plant?" she grinned, making a shoving-up-arse gesture with her arm.

"Yes," he sighed, suddenly even more tired, realising he wanted to be at home doing old fogey stuff, listening to Dvorak or watching Mastermind. Even watching a blank screen. Or down the pub. Or, yes, down at the launderette. Anywhere. "Yes, I'll look after everything."

"I can't go back to my friends. I don't have any friends, and they're all off their heads anyway."

"You've been drinking too, haven't you?"

"A little vodka."

"That's just awful. You know, I had my first beer when I was eighteen."

"Yes but you're an old fella. You grew up in history."

"I am twenty five."

"That's fucking ancient."

"On the contrary, that is very young. Which makes you extremely young indeed. Particularly to be drinking vodka."

"You could report me. But then you'd have to report the whole fucking school."

"You know, you really should moderate your language, it's very unladylike."

"I'm not a lady," she retorted, in a new tone, suddenly a rather cold and crisp manner. He noticed that, the chilliness. And wondered vaguely why. Why had she clicked from one mood to another, as if by a switch? He looked at her, carefully. And she looked back, everything about her saying yeah, so what?

"Drink and language," he said, shaking his head, " it's just up to you. You have to learn to self discipline yourself." He looked away. Something about those weird eyes were slightly intimidating. Also her low cut top. His eyes would tend to drift down there. Nature's way, and that. And he knew she'd notice, and wait for it, and mock him in some way. That'd give her some advantage, if she saw him looking down her front. "Self discipline," he continued, looking away from her and towards the dancers, "it's up to you. At your age. It's no good teachers and principals trying to lay down the law. It's a personal responsibility."

"Oh God shut up I don't need a lecture."

"You mustn't tell teachers to shut up. It's quite disrespectful. It doesn't affect the teacher, but it does reflect badly on yourself."

"Just bleeding fucking shut up then," she screeched suddenly, and then was quiet, equally suddenly. This kid is off her head, he realised. He looked around, grateful just in that moment that the noise was so bad, no-one else seemed to have heard the outburst.

"You're upset," he said, reaching out his hand, to touch her on the elbow, that sort of gesture. But the hand he reached out held the plant, and he stopped his arm, just there.

"You're giving me the plant?"

"No, I was going to…"

"Touch me."

"Yes," he admitted. "Just on the elbow," he added quickly. "But." He waved the plant, and smiled. "And," he swayed the bucket in his other hand. "Just don't have any hands available."

"You could put that stuff down. And touch me." Her mood had shifted from screeching harridan to flirtatious. This is not a girl, he told himself. This is a little chemical time bomb standing here in front of me, waiting to go off.

"The moment has passed," he said, looking cooly at her. Like

126

he might look at a grown up woman of his own age. Look here, he told himself, there's no point in treating these kids as children. Particularly when they're on drugs. Deal with them on their own level. They hate that, usually.

"The moment? For touching me?"

"You're not upset anymore." He didn't like the way the conversation was going.

"Do you only touch women when they're upset?"

"You are not a woman," he started to say, realising that he liked even less the way the conversation was going.

"Oh," she said, doing something with her shoulders that affected the lie of her breasts. Something far from subtle with her shoulders.

"No, you are not." Time for firmness, he told himself. I am the boss in this situation. "Look," he raised his hand to emphasise. Though the wilting plant he held didn't really help the moment. "Look, you are a schoolchild, you are drunk, and more than that, I suspect. On something. And I am a teacher and I'm telling you, you should really go home."

"We could go up on the balcony," she said.

*

SUSSEX POLICE. ARUN DISTRICT. BOGNOR SOUTH.
TRANSCRIPT.
14.15. 20 March
DI HARRIS - John Stanley Dexter

"Well here we go again. Nice lunch?"
"So so."
"Good. Now. Let's talk about that balcony John."
"Balcony?"
"Balcony."
"OK. The school hall, it had a balcony around the edges. On three

sides."

"Only three?"

"One end of the hall was the stage."

"What was the balcony for?"

"Watching plays and so on. Also the lights for the stage, the spotlights and equipment and that, they were up there."

"Watching plays?"

"Yes but the school didn't use it for that anymore. Just had become a discipline problem. Kids up there would be out of sight. Smoking. Up to god knows what."

"What did you think, when she said the two of you could go up on the balcony."

"Well what would you think?"

"I would think she was making a pass at me."

"That's what I thought too. But we're trained to expect that. From young teenage girls. They test out their sexuality on teachers."

"You're trained?"

"To deflect inappropriate behaviour. Without of course damaging the girls' self esteem."

"Of course. Naturally. Right. Get you. Though that's all psychological mumbo jumbo politically correct crap, isn't it?"

"Well it can be a very difficult area."

"Difficult. Um. Young girl. Short skirt. Nice thighs. Wants to put it about a bit. How difficult is that?"

"I didn't say she had nice thighs."

"Listen. She had nice thighs. Face facts. Nice thighs leading all the way up to a nice little arse. And nice little breasts up on top. Cherries on the cake. You didn't mention them'.

"I didn't mention her thighs either."

"I don't listen to words."

"So why ask questions?"

"To get answers. Answers don't come in words, mate. They come in silence. In between the words."

"Really?"

"Yes, really. Dumb policemen are taught stuff like that. You might say we were trained. Just like brilliant schoolteachers are trained. To stop young girls taking their knickers off."

"Whatever."

"Or are the teachers trained to stop themselves, to stop themselves taking their pupils' knickers off?"

"It's a balanced approach. Training recognises the potential for inappropriate behaviour on all sides of the equation."

"Does it indeed. So let's put that in English. It says keep your dirty mitts off the young girls, or you'll end up in front of fuckers like me, thick cops who'll give you a hard time?"

"I don't think you're thick."

"Well, there's one thing we agree on. So. Here we have it. Young teacher. Young wife at home. Young girl on balcony. Quick shag. I understand these things."

"You don't. And I didn't have a wife, then. Yvette was in Belgium."

"What was she doing in Belgium?"

"Getting things ready. For the wedding."

"Getting things ready? For the wedding? In Belgium? And you're shagging this underage girl in Walthamstow? Oh John. John John John."

"I wasn't."

"So you say. But anyway. Tell me more… about this balcony."

"It's just sort of, up there. Like a mezzanine."

"A mezzanine?"

"Between the floor of the hall, and the roof. A sort of extra floor."

"I know what a fucking mezzanine is. I want to know about the balcony. Like how do you get there?"

"Up a stairs. Two stairs actually. Two ways up."

"Where are these stairs?"

"Where?"

"Like where do they start from?"

"One is from the corridor. Outside the hall."

129

"And the other?"

"From outside the building altogether. That's an escape route really. Fire regulations."

"So you can't go up that?"

"Well you can, but you can't get in."

"Can't get in?"

"There's one of those escape bars, inside, so you can only open the doors from inside."

"Though if someone had propped it open."

"Well then you could get in."

"And this other stairs, from the corridor?"

"What about them?"

"Someone could go out into the corridor. Or, some people, like say two people, or more precisely two people sneaking off for an illicit rendezvous…"

"An illicit rendezvous?"

"Yeah, I like the phrase, glad you appreciate."

"But a rendezvous is a place you meet. Two people wouldn't go together to it. Unless they were meeting someone else. They'd go seperately. To the rendezvous. If there was only two of them."

"I'll remember that. When I'm doing my fucking A levels English."

"It's French. Rendezvous. Anyway they wouldn't ask you questions like that. Grammar is a dead duck."

"Got you. Dead ducks. Thing is, John, I tend to worry more about dead people than dead ducks. It's my area, of expertise, so to speak. So. Moving right along. You're telling me, you can sneak out of this hall, into the corridor, and up a stairs to the balcony."

"I didn't say anything of the sort."

"You can sneak out, and up to the balcony, unseen by the people in the hall, right?"

"Yes you could, but I didn't say you could."

"If you wanted to, you could. Did you want to?"

"Want to what?"

"Go up on the balcony with the girl."

"Didn't cross my mind."

"You mad, or gay, or both?"

"It wasn't appropriate."

"Appropriate. You mean some old fuckers or some old biddys wrote it down in a book, an instructional manual for young teachers."

"Well it would be general...sort of policy...accepted in our culture. And particularly in schools. It's really quite a betrayal. Of the kids."

"But it's general policy of your balls to be heading towards young women. Human nature."

"But that's what civilisation is all about, taking human nature, adapting it to life, so to speak. Social mores. Without discipline and values what would we have?"

"We'd have modern England, wouldn't we? Lookit, I'm not going in this direction. Social mores my arse. I'm too old for philosophy. Any conversation with social mores in it has gone too far."

"You brought it up."

"Did I? OK. My fault. So. So you went up on the balcony with the girl?"

"I didn't say that."

*

"The balcony?," he asked her, "why should we go up there?

She shrugged. A one shoulder shrug. A peculiar sort of shrug, perhaps more like a twitch than a shrug. Something nervous about the gesture. But whatever it was like, John Dexter realised what it said. If you have to bloody ask then there's not much point anyway.

"I'll just leave the rubbish in the cleaners' cupboard," he said, " I'll let them know about it tomorrow."

"We could bring the bucket to the balcony."

"I don't see the point, really." He wondered what was that she was on, that something on top of the vodka. It'd be good to know the symptoms, of the different drugs. They live in a bit of a secret world, these kids. Stuff we were taught about in college probably completely old fashioned by now. He wondered about the drugs. Apart from weed...ok and a bit of acid in Sussex University days... he didn't really have any experience himself. But he knew there was definitely something there. Though she didn't actually appear to have any symptoms, nothing manic, or hyper, or twitchy. Outside those sudden flips of mood she was, in fact, very calm. Maybe she was just mad. The only certainty was that she was quite drunk.

"We could drop the stuff over onto the dancers," she said, calmly, pointing at the bucket.

"Why would we do that?"

"It'd be fun."

"But it could hurt someone. There's bits of rocks and shards of pottery. Someone could get a nasty gash."

"Yes," she agreed, seemingly none too perturbed about the possibility.

"Is there someone has annoyed you, that you want to dump rubbish on their head?" he wondered.

"No, not particularly, a lot of people there are my friends."

"Ah but you said you hadn't any friends," he challenged.

"People I know," she responded. "But people who don't know me. Do you call them friends?"

"I don't think it's the time of night for that sort of discussion. It's interesting but..."

"What is it the time of night for?"

"Certainly not the time of night for dropping stuff on your friends' heads." He smiled, and she didn't smile back. "Or on the heads of people you know, but who don't know you."

She still didn't smile, but looked at him intensely. A lot more intensely than he would have expected, with the vodka and drugs and whatever else. That look reminded him of some animal behind a bars, in a zoo. There's a moment when it suddenly catches your eyes. And you realise that you haven't a clue who is in there. This was that moment. It shook him up a little, unnerved him a bit.

I don't want to look into this girl's eyes, he realised.

She'll draw me in. And I'll drown. And I'll end up on a sex register.

He looked away.

"Isn't it interesting," she asked, "that you wouldn't know where it would fall, the rubbish, or on who. Not in the dark with the noise and the dancing, it'd be all down to chance."

"Chance?"

"It's the same like you never know who you're going to meet, do you, Mr Dexter? Get up in the fucking morning. Think it's another fucking day. But it's a different day, innit. Something's going to happen. Some fucker's going to stand behind you in the tube, push you under a train. They do that, you know. Mad fuckers. You never know if they're standing behind you. Like you can't look behind you all the time. You've got to take a chance. It's your fate, or not your fate."

"You really should go home. Do you want me to get Miss Wilson to take you home?"

"Miss Wilson can fuck herself. With that brush. Do her good."

"It doesn't do you any good you know, being angry."

"I'm not angry. I'm talking about fate. And destiny. And getting up in the morning. And not knowing what's going to happen. Who you're going to meet. You didn't know you were going to meet me today, did you?"

"No."

"I knew I was going to meet you."

This girl is a psychiatric case, Dexter thought. Is there no counselling or social workers or child protection people or whatever in bloody Walthamstow? What the hell is a half dressed teenage girl doing being let wander around like this? Out of her bloody head.

What will happen to her?

"How did you know," he asked gently. Gently because he felt gentle towards her, now. And her eyes were lovely and her feet were pretty. "How did you know," he asked, "how did you know you were going to meet me?"

"Fate. Don't you believe in fate, Mr Dexter? Destiny? Our destiny?"

Further chapters of THE COLOUR OF HER EYES may be accessed
(for free!)
via the author's website
www.conankennedy.com
(That site will also link you to international reviews of the book).

The entire book (ISBN 9780907677741)
is available (around $US 3.00) for all eBook readers' systems,
Kindle, Sony, Nook etc
via Amazon and other providers.
Email morriganbooks@gmail.com
for details of printed book availability.

An extract from
Conan Kennedy's

THE SNAKE
DANCER OF
SATI CHOURA

Introduction

My name is Arthur Doyle. I am a medical doctor in the county of Monaghan, a remote, impoverished and somewhat backward region of Ireland. Here I run a large hospital in one of the major towns. Before I moved into the administrative area I was a consultant specialist in geriatrics, and this remains an area of medicine in which I have a particular interest. I feel that I can state, (hopefully without too much affront to modesty), that I do have a certain affinity with and expertise in dealing with older people.

In recent years, while not clinically involved in their care any more, I have maintained that interest. I feel this interest has not been to the detriment of my other responsibilities. In my administrative inspections and tours of wards and units within the hospital I do make a conscious effort to apply equal attention to paediatrics, surgical, medical and all the areas that fall within my remit. It must be admitted that I am perhaps forced to make that particular 'conscious' effort because I have noted that, in my 'managerial wanderings' around our complex, I have inevitably ended up in our geriatric wards chatting to the patients.

However, I fail to find it necessary to recriminate with myself for this apparent 'bias'. Indeed, on the contrary, and again hopefully without too much affront to modesty, I feel that I am amply fulfilling the demands imposed upon myself by both the Hippocratic Oath and by my own firmly held Christian convictions. It is a sad commentary on our society that our older citizens are so ignored by the 'generality', if I may apply that word to our younger people who in fact form, essentially, a minority. Our older citizens are, in fact, the 'generality'. A demographic, statistical and perhaps technical point admittedly, but one perhaps worthy of restating.

It would be untrue to state that I am 'amazed', in that little amazes *me at this stage of a long career, but nonetheless I do 'note', and am perhaps 'surprised' at how few visitors our geriatric patients receive. Very frequently I discover that I am the only person to whom an individual might have spoken throughout the day. Or indeed, throughout a week. In this context I mean the word 'speak' to be understood in the non-medical sense. Our nurses and doctors are excellent. It goes without saying that I wouldn't countenance otherwise. The ship I run is, as our American friends are wont to say, tight. My staff are competent, and friendly and open, and would of course give a few minutes of non-medical attention to the elderlys' care. I define 'non-medical' in the sense of normal friendly human banter and intercourse. I here use the terms 'medical' and 'non-medical' in the sense that the lay person might understand, but essentially (in a medical sense!) there is no difference. (My senior colleagues will forgive me for pointing that out and younger members of our profession could, I feel, do worse than refer to my paper on the topic in* The Lancet*).*

That then is the preamble. My exposition above hopefully explains how I met and became friendly with one of our geriatric patients. I find it unnecessary to include her name here, privacy is a dignity too often denied our elderly.

This lady had come into our care from what is euphemistically referred to as a 'nursing home', where she had lived previously for five or six years. Prior to which she had lived many years in Dublin with her husband. And there was some talk of India. I recall her mentioning that topic once, but she didn't elaborate afterwards at our further meetings. I didn't press her on the matter, feeling that she had decided not to discuss India. When widowed, she had returned to Monaghan, her native place. And indeed a place where she had earlier inherited the family farm. It had fallen into dereliction in her decades of absence but she restored it, and created a successful business in the breeding and raising of rare breed poultry for export to the Asian market. She did not seem to have been short of money. Then, when age and infirmity had caught up, as indeed it does to us all (a fact too often forgotten), she sold up and moved into the nursing home. And thence, as noted, after five or six years, she came to us. She was well into her eighties at this stage, but completely compis, and well aware of her surroundings. It must be stated, however, that she did not actually pay much attention to her surroundings. Instead she lay there, or sat there, quietly, elsewhere in her mind. One knew her gaze was on distant things. But she always greeted me warmly. With phrases like "ah, the good doctor arrives," accompanied by a warm smile and a twinkle of her eyes. I rather think she took a fancy to me, if I might be so presumtuous. But the very elderly sometimes do, a younger doctor or a nurse reminding them of a husband or a wife from distant times.

The lady's husband had been a writer. Of the middle rank, I gathered, and not particularly successful or well known. All professions are, of course, akin to armies, in that there are more 'foot soldiers' than generals. The medical profession is no exception to this phenomenon. Many doctors are in that 'foot soldier' category, competent, professional, jacks of all trades, and able to make a satisfactory living in an anonymous sort of way. Few enough of us can rise to be directors of large medical facilities. Hopefully without being flippant I can suggest that doctors such as myself are the 'best sellers' of our profession.

My patient knew she was dying. We discussed death and the hereafter and, wearing my other hat as Lay Preacher with the First (Reformed) Church of Christ (Redeemer), I feel I did manage to at least raise an awareness of The Lord's promises and the certainty of Salvation and Eternal Life in the Divine Presence of the Christ Jesus. For my own part I did find prayerful consolation in observing the serene way she smiled at my words.

It was at one of our last meetings that she gave me this, the manuscript of the book that follows. She told me that her husband had published many books but, as is the way with professional writers, there were many that remained unpublished. And of most of these she said they are merely notes and passing thoughts, and will make the good startings of a fire for somebody. But this particular one, she said, it would be nice if it saw the light of others' days. 'Nice' was precisely the word she used. And equally, 'the light of others' days' was precisely the phrase she applied. I recall that without hesitation. Since my student days, and hence perhaps my success in my field, I have been renowned for the precision of my memory. A gift of God, of course, and to be appreciated for that. An appreciation which, it goes without saying, should always be accompanied by an understanding that a gift from God is a tool from God, a tool to carry out His work.

When giving me this manuscript she did not say, or ask, or request that I organise its publication. She merely said, and I quote again, it would be nice if it saw the light of others' days. After some thought and consideration and, indeed, after a seeking of God's guidance, I have found that to be a sentiment with which I can concur.

* * *

One

The guy was a fucking nerd. Or a geek. Never too sure of the difference. One thing certain though. If he was a nerd he was a nerd's nerd. And if a geek? Yes, he was a geek's geek.

Thing about nerds. And geeks. Keep them on topic. They're specialists. That's what they're there for, created for. They know things, useful things. But these are not the sort of things a man wants to clutter up his mind with. The things geeks know are things that come in handy on a particular occasion. Useful for a particular purpose. And afterwards best forgotten. Remember that, all goes well.

Summary. With nerds avoid the generality. And avoid the specifics outside the nerd's speciality. Politics and sex, avoid. No point. Your nerd is a Nazi. Or a Green. He wants to kill jews and blacks. Or he wants to save the planet. His political ideas and ambitions are deranged, psychotic, and dangerous. He's an extremist. And as for sex. Jeez. Avoid that definitely. Like plague, avoid it. Your nerd stroke geek is weird in this department of the human condition. I mean all us blokes like to dress up in frilly lingerie now and then... but your nerd? No, you do not want to go there. Auto eroticism? Partial strangulation? Dressing up as that little girl star of silent Charlie Chaplin movies? No harm in any of that. We've all done it. But all at the same time? Normal, for a nerd.

"Tell me about the photograph" I said to him.

"Well," he pointed. At the photo. "Like what do you want to know?"

"How did it come about? Starters. How did you meet him, how'd he get in touch with you?"

"Guy at work. Knew a guy. Who knew a guy."

"Uh huh," I said, my code for please-continue.

"Did you know that if you walk up to a stranger in New York he will know someone who will know someone who..."

"Yes," I interrupted, "I do know that." I also know that if you walk up to a stranger in New York and start talking he could take out a legally held firearm and shoot you.

"Interesting isn't it?"

"Not overwhelmingly," I had to tell him, putting a firm fullstop to that line of chatter. "Let's move it on a bit. So, guy at work. This guy knew someone who knew someone who knew someone who knew that this was your area of...area of what?"

"Expertise?"

"He put you in touch?"

"Uh huh."

"Where'd you meet?"

"At the crepèrie in Stephens Green Shopping Centre"

"At the crepèrie in Stephens Green Shopping Centre?"

"What's wrong with that?"

"Funny place to meet."

"Where would you meet?"

"Depends."

"On what?"

"Who I was meeting. And for what purpose. Like if I was meeting a woman..."

"Do you have a woman?"

"Good question," I replied.

Good question.

I thought of her. Brown hair, pale shoulders, brown eyes, short sighted.

"Thinking of getting my eyes lasered," the brown eyed girl said to me.

"For what?"

"To see better."

"What do you want to see better?"

"The world."

"Not a good idea," I told her.

She laughed. I played with her brown hair. Drawing patterns with it on her pale shoulders. Good memory. Good question. Did I have a woman?

"What's it to you?" I said to the nerd.

He shrugged. "Just making conversation."

I shrugged.

So what do we have? Two men shrugging at each other in the bar of the Shelbourne Hotel. Good place to meet though. Quiet in the morning. Free nuts. I ate some. Problem with free nuts is there's a lot of free crap in the bowl as well, to bulk it out. Crap equals bulk. They teach them that in the catering business. So a guy's got to poke around in this crap to find a pistachio. Recession I suppose.

What is that crap anyway?

Some of it's pink.

What does it matter?

Do I have a woman?

Silent questions. A man looking for the lone pistachio in a bowl of nuts but mostly crap comes across a lot of questions in his mind. Silent questions. Best to break that silence.

"Why did you meet him, in the crepèrie, in Stephens Green Centre?"

The nerd didn't answer. OK, time to reveal. He had a name. James. So, James didn't answer. He just pointed at the photo on the table.

Grafton Street. From the top, looking down. Mid morning sort of photograph. Busy enough, but not frenzy busy. And not like one of those photos the media uses to illustrate the state of the economy. Out of focus faces with shopping bags swinging around knees, those sort of images. Not like that at all.

"This is a good photo," I told James.

Keep your nerd onside.

They have certain sensitivities.

Can go bad on you, unexpectedly, your nerd.

"How do you mean?"

"Well, like he's in focus, and everyone else sort of fades into the distance."

"I'm a photographer."

"Yeah but when I take a photo everyone remains in focus. Foreground, background. If I took that photo it'd be in focus right down to the end of the street. Why is that?"

"Just the way you set the camera. And also of course the fact that you don't know what you're doing."

"I suppose so."

I looked at the photo.

He was tall, not too tall. Goodlooking, not too goodlooking. Well dressed, not too...all that.

"Funny thing," I said to James.

"What, what's funny thing?"

"Hey look I found a pistachio."

"That's funny?"

"No not really, That's an aside. But funny too, I suppose. In a way...here am I looking at the photo and my fingers in the bowl find their own pistachio. Without me looking, like. Know what I mean?"

"Uh huh."

"The real funny thing though, about photography."

James looked at me, waiting. He had close cropped hair. I wondered if he was gay. But what did it matter to me?

Good to know though.

Facts like that can come in useful, later.

"The funny thing about photography is..." I paused, to let him know that there was an insight coming up. And it might very well be to his advantage to listen, carefully.

He listened, carefully.

If, I told him, if I look down Grafton Street the whole street will be in focus. Yeah admittedly stuff in the distance does get smaller. And hard to make out. Hard to read shop signs. Recognise faces. But it still will be in focus. Ever think of that?

"Of what?"

"That. Why do photographers focus their photo."

"It's an art form. Photography."

"And looking down the street with eyes isn't?"

"Eyes actually do focus anyway," he said, "but in a sort of intellectual way."

"You wha?"

"They choose what to see, pick out what's relevant. Ignore all the peripheral."

"But the peripheral is still in focus."

"You can actually focus your ears," James said.

"Can I?"

"Ever been in a crowded pub?"

"No never, against my religion."

"Well in a crowded pub and everyone chattering and you look across at someone you're interested in..."

"Like someone you fancy?" I interrupted. Kind of thinking James needed all the interruptions he could get.

"Not necessarily. But that too. And you focus your ears and hear what they're saying."

"But your ears don't move."

"What's that got to do with it?"

"Nothing, nothing."

I picked up the photograph. I didn't want to look at it anymore, just wanted to talk about it. And picking something up...the very holding an object sort of helps the mind to concentrate.

Wonder why that is?

I suppose other senses kick in. Senses of which we have no comprehension and why should we? Does a computer know it's a computer? Or a washing machine, does a washing machine know it's a washing machine? No, it just washes.

Computers compute, washing machines wash.

Deal with it.

"He came to you," I told him, told James the photographic nerd, "he came to your office..."

"Studio," he interrupted.

"He came to your studio and told you he wanted a photograph. A particular photo. This photo. A photo of him walking up Grafton Street."

"Uh huh."

"But not just anywhere, not anywhere in Grafton Street."

"No, a particular point."

"Let's go there." I stood up. One last poke around in the nuts. All crap now. Nothing edible. "Let's go there. I'll be you and you be him."

"Come again?"

"Show me what he did."

"But we weren't coming from the Shelbourne Hotel."

"What's that mean?"

"Well we came up the street, up Grafton Street."

"Your gaff is in Aungier Street."

"My studio, yes."

"Why would you come up Grafton Street from Aungier Street? Would you not come along by the Gaiety, South King Street, along there."

"We weren't coming from the studio."

"I know." I sighed. Oh god. This was getting exhausting. Already. "I know. You were coming from the crepèrie in the shopping centre."

"Why'd you raise the point then?"

"It's what I do. Check things. Give people opportunity. To change their stories."

"To catch them out. Because you're a cop?"

"I am an investigator."

"But you were a cop."

"I have been many things"

"What's that mean?" he asked. But I didn't answer immediately. Because just at that precise moment I entered the swing door of the hotel and had a sudden flashback of those circular packets of cheese we had as kids. Circular, divided into trangular segments of cheese. And those segments were just like the compartments inside swing doors. Segments which in some cases were all the same type of cheese, but in other cases the packet offered a variety. Some spreadable, some called Galtee, and others Mitchelstown. Named for different cheese manufacturing localities. Yeah they all tasted the same, but what do kids know about cheese? Point is, they all had different labels.

"What do you mean," James asked again as he came out of the door behind me, "what do you mean you've been many things?"

"I've been a son and a lover," I told him, "and a man standing beside a grave. Many things. I've been the story and the storyteller, many things."

"That why they threw you out of the police?" James asked.

"Why what."

"Because you're crazy?"

"Sanity is a greatly overrated condition," I told him. "And anyway they didn't throw me out. I took early retirement."

"How old are you now?"

"Thirty four."

"How long have you been out?"

"About six years."

"I see what you mean" said James. "Early retirement."

"Let's move" I told him.

We walked along the Green to the top of Dawson Street, and then down, so that we could cut across and walk up Grafton Street to the location of the photo.

"What time was it?" I asked, "the time of the photo."

"Around now."

I looked at my watch. Phillipe Patek. Twenty dollars on a street corner in New York. Can't get a good watch much cheaper.

Eleven fifteen.

"Was that time specific, chosen, or was it just circumstance?"

"Oh no, he choose the time of the photo. Well, not exactly. Not to the minute. But he said between eleven and half past. Mid morning."

"Mid morning?"

"Well he didn't actually say that, he said half way between breakfast and tiffin."

"Tiffin?"

"I asked him that too. It means lunch. In India."

I looked at the photo. "He doesn't look Indian to me."

"He wasn't. White bloke."

"So why's he talking Indian?"

"Hindi. Or Urdu," said James. "There's no such language as Indian. Though I suppose English is a general language all over. And maybe that could be called Indian."

"Thank you for that input. What I mean is, why's he using a foreign word anyway?"

"Ask him," said James.

"I will," I promised. "When I find him." Then thought about the thing for a moment. "Strange way of putting it though" I suggested. "I mean saying between breakfast and tiffin or saying between breakfast and lunch…still strange."

"He was a strange bloke."

"What do you mean *was*? Is he dead?"

"Why would he be dead?"

"Why not? In the midst of life we are in death. We have not here a lasting city."

"I meant *was*, like when he *was*, *was* with me, he was strange then."

"You *perceived* him as strange."

"Exactly."

"And you don't know whether he's alive or dead now?"

"How would I know, he was just a client. Might have been run over by a bus since. In London."

"Why London?"

"Just London. People go to London."

"Did he go to London?"

"I don't know where the fuck he went. And I don't really care."

"I care."

"It's your job to care."

"Caring is not a job," I told him, "it's an emotion."

I felt good about this remark. So I elaborated. Thinking I'd maybe feel even better if I spun it out a bit. "That's the problem with this world. Everything is jobs, and bought and sold. So we end up with things like professional carers. Like being a professional hooker isn't it?"

"Isn't what?"

"Like why does a man go to a prostitute?"

"I have no idea," said James.

Yeah, I thought, looking at his close cropped hair, yeah he's probably telling the truth there.

"Well I'll tell you then. People go to prostitutes because they can't get that service at home. And they have to go out and pay for it. Same with carers. Our society is not providing care. So we have to have professional carers. Same difference."

"Oh for fuck's sake," said James.

He was probably right.

We walked along Anne Street. I wondered why he was leading

me there and I asked him. Because Anne Street is not at the bottom of Grafton Street, and if we walked up from there we'd be missing a whole area. But James explained that no, it didn't matter. Because the day he took the photo the client had just hurried along until quite near the top of Grafton Street. Like he knew the general location. And only got specific in the last fifty yards or thereabouts. Well that's what James said. Though maybe he was sick of me and my philosophy, and wanted to hurry things along.

It happens.

From the intersection of Anne and Grafton we walked up the street, James gradually walking slower and...slower...and slower. All the while looking around, in a distracted sort of concentration.

If he was painted silver folks would have been giving him money, that sort of walk.

"What are you doing, precisely?" I asked, politely.

It seemed a reasonable question.

"Well you said, you be him and I be you. I'm being him."

"OK. OK. But you could just say he slowed down round here, and looked around. Like he was searching."

"Remembering. He looked around like he was trying to remember."

"You know the difference?"

"The word just came to me."

"He was looking for a specific place. And you're acting out the part. You ever think of going into acting?"

"No, do you think..."

"No," I interrupted. "The words day job. Give up. Don't. Make your own sentence."

James stopped.

I stopped.

Pedestrians walked round us like we were a rock and they were the tide. But they took no heed of us nor we of them. It was automatic, that walking round us.

"Here," he said, right here.

"How do you know?"

"Because this is where he stopped."

"How do you know, how do you remember? Like one part of the street looks much like another."

"It's the patterns on the street. Those lines of brick. Different colours."

"Paviors they call those bricks," I told him.

"How do you know that?"

"I know a lot of things."

"OK. Those lines of brick." James pointed. "Those ones up there, too far. Those ones down there, not far enough. These ones..." He pointed at our feet. "Just right."

"I don't get it James."

"What don't you get?"

I told him. The guy had been taking him to a spot, a specific spot. And a specific place is by definition a place that someone knows, knows beforehand. So why all this looking around, this searching, this remembering? Why that?

James didn't know.

He just shrugged. *Way it is*, that shrug told me. I can read a shrug. Not too difficult. *Way it is*, that's what most shrugs say. Though some say *I don't care*. Language of shrugs. A science in itself.

Like eyes, the language of eyes. Though much more complex that, that particular language. The way she looks at you. In the morning. How different is that to the way she looks at you in the evening? Is it different at all? You want it to be different. But in a good sort of way. Good different. Not bad different.

Did I have a woman?

I wondered, standing there like a rock in the street and a tide of pedestrians washing round me. It seemed to take a while, that wondering, about the woman. But maybe it wasn't that long at all. Maybe only a minute, or two. It just seemed a while of wondering.

There's a lot of thoughts about a woman, a particular woman, a lot that a man can get into his mind in a short time, wondering.

It passed, the daze. And I became aware of James the nerd photographer beside me, watching, waiting.

"So this is where he stood" I said.

"Right there."

"There? Not here?"

"I meant there where you are standing, not me."

"We're kind of close together, what's the difference?"

"I don't know. He just stood there. And I stood here."

"No you didn't."

"What do you mean?"

"You went up there and took the photo."

"Yeah of course. But you know what I mean."

"I don't know what anything means. So ok. Now I'll be you and you be me. Or, more precisely, you be him, and I'll be you, I'll take the photo. How far up the street did you go?"

"Next line of coloured bricks."

"Ok I'll go up there and look back."

I went up there and looked back.

James was standing, facing me. No, not standing. He was posing. Just like one of those silver painted guys who make a living as human statues, whatever they call themselves. Standing like he was walking, no, not walking, strolling. Right hand in his pocket, and left hand loose by his side.

I recognised the stance.

Guy in the photo stood like that.

James was acting out a part. And enjoying himself, this little outing. Perhaps he didn't get out that much, meet enough interesting guys like me. A lonely life. Being a nerd. A gay nerd. Lonelier.

I looked at him.

People ignored us, what did they care? We were two rocks now and they were the tide. Same tide, different rocks. What does the tide know of the rocks except to flow around? And wash away in time? That's all, that's all the tide needs to know. But the rocks, the rocks need to know a lot more. Like where to stand and who to love, what other rock to love. Needs to know all that, your rock.

But your average rock?

Knows diddley squat, your average rock, just stands there in the tide.

Wondering, do I still have a woman?

Thinking, something wrong.

Looking at James back there in the street and that way he was standing in a vaguely mad looking fashion. But what did it really matter? Most folks in Grafton Street are standing or walking in a vaguely mad looking fashion, it's the human condition.

No, it wasn't that, it wasn't that which was wrong.

I walked back down to him.

"You're imitating the guy in the photo, right?"

"Yeah, how am I doing?"

"Not bad," I congratulated, "but not quite."

I stood beside him, to his left.

"Hold my hand," I told him.

I suppose he blushed. Being of that persuasion. Or, indeed, not being of that persuasion. Like if he was gay as pink ink he'd blush, and if he wasn't, likewise. Though I suppose it'd be a different sort of blush.

Language of blushes?

Reckon so.

I held his hand. And then I said "hey, I'm going to let go of your hand."

"Yeah maybe you should, people are looking."

"Fuck them. I'm going to let go of your hand but I want to you to keep your hand in precisely this position."

"Got you."

I let go of his hand and walked back up the street and looked back.

Yes, that was it. James was standing as if he were holding someone's hand. No, not standing. Not exactly. Standing in a walking position, as if frozen. Frozen in the midst of strolling up Grafton Street holding someone's hand. Just like the guy in the photograph had stood.

Why hadn't I noticed that in the photo?

No reason, can't notice everything.

And that wasn't the question anyway. The question was who's hand was the guy in the photo holding. When I knew that I would find him. His name was Richard Roe.

"Where'd you get the photo anyway?," James asked me as we finished up. Or as we started, whatever it was we were doing.

"From my client, Amanda Blake."

I watched him carefully as I spoke, to see if the name might mean anything to him. Hard to tell, hard to tell. He just shrugged and said "And who is she, and what's her interest?"

Good question.

Two

Fifty, sixty, I met her at a wedding. Someone's aunt, I thought, there's always someone's aunt at a wedding. I don't know where they go when there's not weddings on. Particular apartment blocks I suppose, full of someone's aunts, fifty, sixty, that vintage. Yep, it follows. They all live in particular designated apartment blocks. Or down the country. Reckon a lot of people's aunts live down the country. They never married. Or they married a farmer. And have spent their lives trying to work out which was worse. And have gotten worried from the calculations. Worried but healthy looking. That's the fresh air. The farming life. Mass on Sunday. Sex on Saturday. And the mirror every day as seasons pass.

We live in times of mirrors, difficult times. Mirrors on the wall, on the TV screen, in magazines. And we see ourselves, and don't see ourselves. And worry worry worry. Yep, these are the times we live in, difficult times, fragmented times. And we protect ourselves by circles, creating circles to move in. Closely knit. Our companions much the same as us. In age, in class, in colour. Maybe it's good, maybe it's not. Maybe the alternative is spending a lot of time with the elderly black. The elderly black working class. The ones with dementia. Maybe, what do I know? If I had answers to these unanswerable questions I'd be a sociologist. Or a statistician. I just dunno. Sociologically speaking, statistically speaking, about the only thing I do know is there's one hell of a lot of someone's aunts at your average wedding.

And I'd noticed this particular one watching me.

In my job I'm very aware of people watching.

This one certainly watched me, noticed me, picked me out, had me in her sights. But she bided her time. She bided her time through the service. She bided her time through the meal. The speeches. And then in the flux and the flow afterwards she came over and sat beside me. I wasn't that pleased. I was working on another guest, a woman with cleavage. I like a woman with cleavage. I like the very word cleavage. It's complex. I like a complex word. To cleave, verb, seems to mean to hold together. But cleavage, noun, seems to mean to hold apart.

If I read things right.

Maybe I don't.

I'm not perfect.

The someone's aunt came over and sat beside me.

It kind of knocked me out of my stride. With the woman with cleavage. And I wasn't that pleased. But there again in a deeper way I was pleased. Because I reckoned that now I'd find out why she'd been watching me, picking me out, holding me in her sights.

"You're the investigator," she told me.

I smiled, non committedly.

Her name was Amanda Blake.

And her eyes said no, you cannot call me Mandy. And she was not just any old someone's aunt. She was Richard Roe's aunt. And she told me her nephew Richard Roe was missing, and she wanted him found. And she opened her someone's aunt's handbag and took out a photo and handed it to me. And I looked at it, a young man walking up Grafton Street. Informative? No. So no comment there then. Then I asked her why, what's it to you? Like has he no parents, no girlfriend, no siblings to be searching? Obvious questions. Like why is it down to an old aunt to be looking for him? Though I didn't say the word 'old' of course. I am a gentleman. But that was my drift.

Richard Roe had no relatives in Ireland. No girlfriend. No siblings, no-one. All he had was Amanda Blake. He was estranged from his parents. And they were in New Zealand. Well one was in New Zealand and the other in India. Can't precisely remember which, should've taken notes. But it probably didn't matter, both parents were seperated and married with new families. And didn't give a bugger. Though Amanda Blake didn't say the word 'bugger' of course. She being a lady. But that was her drift.

Richard Roe wasn't like a son to her, she said, but she had no children of her own in Ireland. And she found herself going through the motions of parenthood. But they hadn't been close. Yes he had contacted her when he came back to Ireland. And she had ended up spotting him the deposit on an apartment, and she suspected that might very well have been the reason for his contacting her. Part of the reason anyway. Though he had in fairness refunded her when he got sorted with a job.

"Back," I asked, "what do you mean back, you said he came back to Ireland?"

Amanda Blake hesitated. Just that fraction. She probably didn't even know that she hesitated. I did. My job to notice. Little things. "He was away," she said.

"Away? Where away?"

"What does it matter?"

"Could be away the same place again."

"In India. He was away in India. Working."

"What did he work at? In India?"

"I don't know."

"Where'd he work in Ireland?"

"Google."

"What'd he do?"

"I.T. Not that I know what that means."

"Of course you do."

156

"Yes of course I do. But I like to play the granny with younger people."

"Why?"

"Saves a lot of hassle."

Hassle, I thought, hassle? Not a very someone's aunt sort of word really. But maybe fifty sixty is the new thirty. Like black is the new beige or something. What do I know?

Richard Roe worked in Google. In I.T. He had an apartment in Smithfield. He was missing. I was to find him. It was a job. There was a recession on. I needed jobs. That's what I know.

"Ok, Miz Blake," I said, "I'll have a go. Can't guarantee anything. Miz Blake" I concluded, repeating the Miz Blake bit. As a sort of hint for her to say "you may call me Amanda."

She didn't.

She handed me her card.

Amanda Blake it said. Yep, I'd expected that. But there was also an unexpected line of foreign type along the bottom. It looked like Arabic, or Hebrew? No, neither. More Eastern? Perhaps. Indian? Could be. I'll check that out, I decided. Maybe ask the guy in the *Kanpur Curry Kitchen* next time I was eating in his place? Yep, I'd do that. Just as soon as my recovery from his last meal was complete.

Amanda Blake lived in Rathgar. Temple Road. But there was no phone number on the card. Why no number? What the fuck use is a business card without a number? I thought about this, reached no conclusion. Except that maybe there was no space, not enough room on the card. That's a reason? Not a good reason. In fact a very bad reason, how much space does a phone number take up? Certainly not as much as the big fancy monogram AB she had on the thing. Granted, nicely done. None of your *Cut Price Copyshop* graphic design here. *Why pay other's prices when you can get this crap here?* No, this was calligraphy. AB. Stylish. Amanda Blake had style. And she also had very nice legs.

I noticed that as she walked away.

Very nice legs. Almost as nice as her line of patter. Why had she hesitated, about India? What was that all about? Interesting. Just like herself. Attractive woman. But fifty sixty I mused ?

I dunno, I dunno.

Then the one with the cleavage came back to the table.

She was from Longford.

It wasn't really that great a wedding.

*

Very next morning I got the LUAS up to Smithfield.

Amanda Blake didn't.

She arrived outside the apartment on one of those rent-a-bikes.

"You a member of the Green Party?" I asked.

"Fucking cobbles," she replied. "If it's not the fucking cobbles it's the fucking tram tracks."

Her fucking surprised me. Hey maybe I'll rephrase that. Her use of the swear word surprised me. But then I noticed that she was wearing black fishnet stockings. And she really had very very nice legs. And her persona sort of re-established itself in my consciousness. I'd gotten misled at the wedding. By the one with the cleavage from Longford. It happens. But fifty sixty? I dunno, I dunno.

"You look different" I said.

"Than what?"

"Than the wedding."

"I don't go to weddings on bikes."

"Oh so you're not a member of the Green Party."

She laughed. She had a very nice laugh. But fifty sixty?

She parked the bike.

She locked the bike.

"They'd take the eye out of your head round here" she said.

"Who?" I glanced around. Most of the local citizens looked like they were heading off to have a double lattee or coming back from one. And some of the male citizens were wearing low slung laptop bags over their shoulders. Rule of thumb. The longer the straps on those bags, like the nearer the knees hangs the manbag, the bigger the jerk.

Take that from me.

I know these things.

"Who?" I asked her again, "who'd take the eye out of your head?"

"Kids," said Amanda Blake. "Feral kids."

"I don't see any kids."

"That's because they're all in the Children's Court over there." She pointed. "When they get bail they'll come out and steal this bike. And Dublin Corporation will slap the cost onto my Visa."

"You've got a certain view of humanity" I told her.

"Once bitten," she announced, "twice shy."

She winked.

"Ah hah," I said. I was getting the impression that Amanda Blake had been bitten more than once. And thinking that shyness might not generally arise.

We went to the apartment.

I'm a southsider. Smithfield is outside my comfort zone. And my mental filing system has it categorized as a derelict square full of horse shit surrounded by derelict buildings and car scrapping guys. But that's an out of date image. A hangover from maybe when I got lost round there twenty years before. Or whatever reason. Anyhow the place is changed. It's now a tidy square full of homosexual looking street furniture surrounded by crisply modern apartment blocks.

Richard Roe lived in one of these. Block C. A whacking great building on the left coming up from the LUAS stop. Block C, I thought, historic name or what. Who said developers had no imagination? Whatever, Richard Roe lived there anyway. Or, to be more precise, and the reason I was there at all, he did not currently reside there. Not that his absence made much difference. There was an empty feeling in the building anyway, as if Roe's apartment was not the only vacant one.

"Kind of eerie isn't it?" I said to Amanda Blake in the lift.

"What, elevators, eerie?"

"No, the building. It feels empty."

"A lot of the apartments are vacant. Since the recession. A lot of the Polacks gone home."

Ah," I said. Thinking. Elevator. Polacks. Those words, Americanisms. But Amanda Blake didn't have an American accent. So why was that? What accent did she in fact have? But what did that matter?

Good to know.

Good to know these things.

Sixth floor. The corridor was empty too, eerie.

I watched her open the door.

"How come you have a key to your nephew's apartment?"

"Why not?"

"My aunts don't have keys to my place."

"I'm his nearest and dearest. And anyway there's a reason. To feed the cat."

"He has a cat? Why doesn't he feed his own cat?"

"When he goes away."

"Where does he go? India?"

"I don't know," she shrugged. "Just away." She shrugged again. That made two shrugs. One shrug for each breast, so to speak. She was a good looking woman. "He gave me the key. To feed the cat."

"You been feeding it since he vanished?"

"No, the cat's dead, for months."

"What happened the cat."

"Got run over by the LUAS," she said, and gazed up at me, her expression daring me to laugh. And as she dared me to laugh her eyes were sparkley and she was biting her bottom lip with her top teeth and it was a very attractive and appealing combination. But fifty sixty? Those there were probably false teeth I decided. And that sort of took the magic out of the occasion.

We went in, she switched a light. It was one of those dimmer switches and came on gloomy. Rheostats, they are, in technical terms. I know these things. She turned it up. Then down a bit. Then up again. Please stop doing that, I thought, but held my peace. She was the boss. I needed the money. Her money.

First impression of the place. He was a tidy bastard, Richard Roe. Or else he didn't come home that much, not enough to muck up his apartment anyway.

"He goes away a lot," said Amanda Blake, a comment on the tidyness. So, I thought, she can read my mind. Already. And is that good or bad?

"Yes, we've established that" I said and she looked at me as if I'd been cheeky and she didn't like it.

I mooched about. Went out on the balcony...what's that church over there? St Michan's? Yeah, probably, most likely. What am I now, a tourist guide?

I went back in.

"Will I make a cup of tea?" asked Amanda Blake. As if to restore cordial relations.

"No, I'm good," I said.

"Just as well, there's no milk."

"OK let's establish this. Where does he go, when he goes away?"

"Work, I suppose."

"But he works for Google. That's down in Docklands."

"Well they're all round the world too, aren't they?"

"I suppose they are," I agreed, "I'll check it out."

"How?"

"Google?"

She laughed, but still and all was watching me. Just like at the wedding, I realised, watching, and biding her time. But for what, I wondered. At the wedding she'd been waiting for the right moment to approach me. That was just the normal working out of a social situation. But now, what was she waiting for now?

I like to know these things.

It helps.

"Talking technology," I said, "I suppose you checked his Facebook?"

"I don't understand Facebook."

I didn't say anything, didn't believe her. And remembered what she'd said at the wedding. That it was less of a hassle to play the old Granny. Uh huh. And maybe it is, maybe it isn't. Maybe in fact it's quite hard work playing the old Granny if you're Amanda Blake. If you've legs like that. And eyes like that. And that attractive laugh. But there again, maybe it's easy. If all the roles you play are roles you play. If you're an actress it's your job, that sort of thing. Comes with the territory. Change your roles like you change your knickers. Yep, something like that, I thought. Then something in my mind remembered. Some girl thing, about a girl I remembered. Almost a joke, but not a joke, useful too. An actress. She had knickers labelled Monday Tuesday Wednesday…days of the week…seven different pairs…

Yep, comes with the territory.

Changing. Knickers and personalities.

If you're an actress.

"You don't understand Facebook?" I said

"No," she shook her head, biting her lip in that fashion of hers. Radiating innocence. That'd be a childlike innocence if her hair wasn't grey, I reckoned. But it'd also be one of those childlike characteristics that'd buy and sell you, couldn't be trusted, not an inch.

What colour, I wondered, what colour was her hair before it was grey? Was it blonde, or brown, or black? Or red? Should be able to tell that from the colour of her skin.

I looked.

She looked back, defiantly, innocently.

"What colour is your skin?" I asked, but not aloud. And now that I asked myself I realised she was not totally a white person. Yes she was white, but she lacked a certain amount of pink. Her features were white, but they lacked...well...a certain amount of white characteristics.

"Lack," I said, but not aloud. Why is it a *lack* to be not totally white? Perspective? Must be that. White bloke's perspective. But it's the only one I've got.

"You'll know me the next time," said Amanda Blake.

"What do you mean?"

"Isn't that what Dubliners say when they find a stranger staring at them?"

"Yeah, they do, and it usually precedes a fight."

"Are we going to fight?"

"Am I a stranger?"

"We ask ourselves a lot of questions."

"Maybe we're looking for a lot of answers."

She nodded at that, and turned away and walked to the window, looked down into the square.

"My bike is not stolen," she reported, "yet."

"Good," I said, watching her. She was wearing sneakers. For the bicycle I suppose. And sneakers don't do anything for a woman's legs. But then, Amanda Blake's legs didn't need anything done for them. Nor did her backside, nor her figure generally.

"You are one good looking woman" I said, but not aloud. But the grey hair kind of...kind of...kind of does whatever grey hair does.

One good looking woman. One good looking woman who doesn't understand Facebook. Yeah, right. One good looking woman who doesn't tell the truth. Hey OK, benefit of doubt. Maybe she really really doesn't, doesn't understand Facebook. It's not important, I do. And I had checked Richard Roe out on line. And learned not much, diddley squat really. He had one of those Facebook pages that say nothing, with no content. Like he'd set it up and then said to hell. This looks like too much crap, hard work, waste of time, all that. I know the feeling. My page is just like that.

But then, I am not Richard Roe.

I'm not an IT guy.

And I'm not working in Google.

So it's OK for me to have nothing to do with Facebook. But it's not OK for him. It's worse than not OK. It's strange, it's weird, it's peculiar, it's ridiculous.

It just doesn't compute.

And why?

Another damn question. And who knows the answer. But relax, I told myself. One door doesn't close but another opens. And a question with no answer can be the answer to another. And so, continuing, moving on. On Richard Roe's page there wasn't even a picture of himself. But there was a picture of one person, one friend.

Amanda Blake.

I thought of it there in his apartment as I was mooching about, going through his stuff, getting the feel of the place, the feel of the man. I thought of that picture of Amanda Blake on Richard Roe's web page. Thought of it, remembered it, pictured the picture in my mind.

Her hair was brown.

Three

S o, she dyes her hair sometimes. What of it? She's a woman, a woman of a certain age. It's irrelevant. The only relevance being that it's a fact. Therefore useful. Because I was kind of short on facts on this investigation.

Summarise. I had the photo she had given me. I had the photoshopping graphic designer that the photo had led me to. I had Richard Roe's apartment sussed out. Three facts. So was it a good idea to make it a four with the fact of Amanda Blake's vanity? Or the fact of Amanda Blake disguising herself?

Maybe put that in as half a fact.

I left the investigation there for a few days.

A few tricky moments had arisen with my girl, my brown eyed girl. Discussing our relationship. And whether I had her or hadn't. Like was our relationship totally based on sex? Or was there something deeper? And what is deeper than sex anyway? Those kind of questions. Those kind of moments. That took sorting. But there were also other reasons I put Richard Roe to one side. It's like plumbing, this game. A guy takes on whatever comes along. Better to have a big list of stuff you can't get around to just yet than being jobless on the dole. So a job comes in, you do a bit, and leave it there for awhile. OK in plumbing the house gets completely fucked and flooded, but in this investigation game there are more positive results. Facts mature in the brain. And they spin out theories. Which in turn evolve into facts. That's the concept.

Reality?

I spent a few days catching up on other work. At this time I had two jobs going. One for a Sunday tabloid. And one for a wholesaler's warehouse in Walkinstown. The newspaper wanted me to find out who was supplying drugs to certain media figures. The warehouse wanted me to find out who was ripping off pallets of canned grocery items. It was much of a muchness which project I found more interesting. Or maybe I mean which I found less interesting. Much of a muchness anyway. In idle moments I would fantasize that it all came together. And by amazing coincidence and happenstance I would discover that the guys who were supplying drugs to certain media figures were also ripping off the canned goods.

Big pay day there.

But that was a fantasy. It wasn't going to happen. Just like my fantasy about the woman in the next door apartment in Pearse Street. That wasn't going to happen either. Pity. Because she would've looked good in that situation. And might have enjoyed it. Once the initial shock had worn off. Pain is very close to pleasure. It's all to do with the brain. There's receptors in there. Chemicals. Electrical impulses.

Nature knows best.

All to do with the brain.

A rare occurance that, in Ireland. Most things here have very little to do with the brain at all. Except with the parts that deal with corruption, deviouness, nepotism and self delusion. Yes I'm talking the Irish media here. This is all to do with who you know and to whom you're related. A closed circle, family ties, mutual interest. Which is good and bad for the investigator. Good? The individuals all hate each other. Bad? Even though they hate each other they know the old saying, hang together or hang seperately.

Hard to penetrate, all that. It's just not feasible to go up to one half a million a year TV presenter and ask him/her who's supplying cocaine to another half a million a year presenter. It won't work. Investigations are top down or bottom up. This one was a bottom up. And thus takes a long time. Because the bottom in the Dublin drugs world is pretty much way down there. Low. And sad and pathetic. Full of people who should be put out of their misery. Move up a few rungs and it's still sad and pathetic. And dodgy. Watch your back. Up a few rungs more, sad and pathetic still. Yes it's always going to be sad and pathetic. But now it's getting dangerous. Which is why at this level of investigation most crime journalists get their information from the police. It's safer, but only so good. The police don't know that much really. And an awful lot of what they do know is about their overtime system. So all you're really going to learn from the average cop is stuff to make him look good, and his bosses bad.

No, an investigator has to get down and dirty on this. Ask the right questions. Make sure the answer isn't a sixteen year old out of his skull on the doorstep.

With a Glock.

*

Question. When does a flyer become a leaflet, and a leaflet become a brochure? Answer. I don't give one flying fuck. But that's the way of the mind. And that was the way of the mind when I got back into the Richard Roe thing. Absurd questions kept appearing out of nowhere. Like incoming North Korean missiles. But, thing about North Korean missiles, their guidance systems are rubbish, but they still explode, in unexpected places.

These incoming questions filled a void. The case was so vague, and ephemeral, and Amanda Blake so suddenly vanished from the scene, that sort of a void. Normally at the start of an investigation the client hassles on the hour, more or less every hour. Just like a housewife does a plumber, watching shit running down her stairs. That sort of urgency. But no, no outside input to get me going on this, just internal. Absurd questions arising.

But there's an upside on this. When a seemingly meaningless and absurd question arises, then something goes on, brainwise. A process ensues. And eventually things happen. Firstly, the I-don't-give-a-flying-fuck response is generated. Secondly, curiosity gets the better of that and various alternative answers are postulated. And then one goes back to the original absurd question. And it makes more sense now.

The process of the human mind is a continual source of wonder and amazement.

Back to the original. The flyer. The particular flyer in question, or the leaflet, or the brochure had been pinned to Richard Roe's anal retentive noticeboard. I had seen it yes, but had gotten distracted by James's business card that I found there. My new mate James the nerd photographer with whom I'd walked up Grafton Street. Distracted, yes, I'd been distracted from the flyer by his business card. But then, James's business card was very distracting indeed.

It was an unwelcome insight into The Mind of The Nerd.

I didn't want to go there. But had no choice, it's the job.

That business card? It started with a B, a letter B. Then continued with an M, a letter M. These were followed by a picture of an eye. Like one of those eyes in Egyptian hieroglyphics. Straight on, looking at you. The Egyptians couldn't draw eyes in profile. Thick enough, your Egyptians. Whatever. The picture of the eye was followed by the word *Valentine*. And that whole arrangement was followed by the word *Graphics*.

I got it.

You couldn't make this one up.

Be My Valentine Graphics.

"The name of your business sucks" I had told him back in the Shelbourne Hotel.

"It's a visual pun."

"So? It sucks on several different levels."

"But my studio is in Aungier Street."

"That's bad enough without picking a crap name for it."

"It's relevant," he protested. "St Valentine's body is in Aungier Street Church."

"Bet he wouldn't be there if he was still alive. Anyway I think it's only his foot or some small body part."

"We'll soon be able to recreate an individual from a single strand of DNA," said James.

"Who's this *we*?"

"Scientists."

"What the fuck we want to recreate individuals for?"

"We don't know yet. There's a law of unintended consequences. Always remember the space race gave us the non-stick frying pan."

"I'll try not to forget that," I concluded the conversation. But couldn't quite deal with the memory of it. It stuck in the brain like the smell of dogshit. Long after you've cleaned your shoes, that smell, it lingers.

But bad thing, good thing.

The memory of the smell of dogshit reminds you to be careful where you walk. And the memory of an absurd conversation reminds you...reminds you...

The flyer/leaflet/brochure had been pinned to James's noticeboard with the same pin as the business card. And I had seen it there on my visit with Amanda Blake. But, equally, I had *not* seen it because it was pinned with the same pin, and was beneath the card, obscured. So better to say I had *noted* it. I'd taken James's card away but pinned the flyer back onto the board and left it there. But it was *noted*.

Now there are two reasons for pinning two pieces of paper to a noticeboard with the same pin. First reason...shortage of pins. Let's think about that. I thought. This involved me closing my eyes and visualising Richard Roe's notice board. In a sort of zooming way. Like I was a Google street camera. First I visualised the LUAS stop. Then Smithfield. Then the Block C apartment block. Then his particular apartment. Then his kitchen. Then the notice board. And no, my inner google camera discovered, there was no shortage of pins. There were, in fact, so many spare pins that Richard Roe had arranged them decoratively around the edges. In a red blue yellow green colour sequence.

This told me two things.

Firstly that Richard Roe needed to get out more. And more importantly that the doubling up of items on the noticeboard was nothing to do with numbers of pins. No, a different reason for using just the one pin applied in this case.

Analysis? Well...two items stabbed with the one pin must have some connection...in the mind of the pinner. It's night follows day.

Examples? The menus of two different takeaway pizza outfits? One pin. And thus a business card for a graphics studio and a flyer for a photographic exhibition...one pin.

Flyer?

Let's nail that. This particular piece of paper was for the *National Photographic Archive*. So it was probably a leaflet. Or even more likely, a brochure. Because the photo archive is up there, high end, posh. And brochures are posh. That archive doesn't do flyers or leaflets. It does brochures. So yes we're just going to have to call this one a brochure. A brochure for an exhibition called *Dublin in The Rare Oul' Times*.

A photographic exhibition down in Temple Bar.

I know Temple Bar.

Advice? Avoid it generally.

And why?

Because it's a district of Dublin which is equivalent to London's Soho. With added drink and anti-social behaviour. A gathering place for the gobshites of Europe, the deluded, and the sad. But, more relevant, it's a place whose denizens are as interested in old photographs as is your average anti-social gobshite. So it may seem strange to have institutions like the *National Photographic Archive* plonked in the middle of such a place? No, not strange at all, not if you know the history.

The history?

The area was intended to be Dublin's cultural quarter. A warren of old streets and alleyways and warehouses, it had become inhabited by the artistic element of society. Well, by secondhand clothes shops, tattoo parlours and squat-like apartments full of people who might write a book/paint a picture/be active in alternative lifestyles. Eat bean salads.

Body piercing was pretty big.

So the powers-that-be took one look at all this, moved in, threw out the artistic element of society, built huge pubs, cobbled the streets, and dropped a few state funded cultural institutions into the joint. And there they stand today like islands in a dream.

I walked down Essex Street.

And there around a bend it stood, like an island in a dream.

The National Photographic Archive.

I went in.

And there behind the counter she stood, yes, like an island in a dream.

Her name was Sara.

I didn't know her name was Sara. Until she told me. Though it turned out it wasn't actually Sara as us mortals conceive of the name. It was Sara pronounced to rhyme with arse, rather than air. She was very friendly and helpful. And had a very nice pour of knockers.

Sara pronounced-to-rhyme-with-arse told me that I was months too late. Months. The exhibition was long over. It had in fact gone the same way as Dublin in the rare oul times itself, and it was...no more. And the photos had all been taken down and dispersed back into the archive.

"Do you have a catalogue of it?" I asked. "Like a listing of the items?"

She did. It wasn't much help. Did what it said on the tin. Just a listing of the items.

"Do you have an illustrated catalogue? You know, with little thumbnails of the exhibits?"

She didn't. And explained that there wasn't really that much point. Because the catalogue was only given out at the actual exhibition. And the pictures were hanging on the walls then and so who wanted to look at a thumbnail of the image? And anyway there was certain budgetry constraints. There was a recession on.

"We're pretty tightly squeezed you know."

I smiled, but inwardly. As mentioned, she had a very nice pour of knockers. And about eight different funny quips concerning busts and bra sizes competed for verbalizing. I rejected them all. It wasn't appropriate. She was a public servant. So I just said "oh." And looked down the list again.

The usual same old same old.

O'Connell Street before the pillar was blown up. The Phoenix Park before the Gough Statue was blown up. Lots of places before they were blown up. And the GPO, blown up. And then lots of places before they fell down. The exhibition seemed to me have illustrated some things well. Like the fact of Dublin's modern history largely consisting of blowing things up. Having a revolution. Throwing out anyone who knew how to keep things together. And then letting anything not already blown up fall down.

I read down the list, nodding. And noted that the exhibition would also have shown me *Urchins swinging out of lamp posts on ropes*. And *Horses and carts*. And *Eccles Street, home to Leopold Bloom, (made famous by James Joyce)*. And *A Day at The Races*. And *Grafton Street in 1896*.

"Grafton Street in 1896" I said to Sarah.

"Oh yes, that, nice photo, we think it's by Bourne."

"Who's we and who's Bourne?"

"Well, we are the keepers. Specialists I suppose."

Further details of
THE SNAKE DANCER OF CHATI CHOURA
will be found via the author's website
www.conankennedy.com

The book is due for publication in June 2012
and will be available
both as a printed book (ISBN 978-0-907677-51-2)
and in eBook format (ISBN 978-0-907677-53-6)
The printed format in Irish bookshops
or directly via PayPal from the author's website,
the eBook via Amazon or the author's website above.
Readers who now register their interest by emailing
morriganbooks@gmail.com
will be alerted when the book is available.

Also by Conan Kennedy

Fiction
HERE BE GHOSTS
OGULLA WELL
THE COLOUR OF HER EYES
THE SNAKE DANCER OF SATI CHOURA
THE GIRL IN THE BUTTERFLY DRESS

Non-fiction
ANCIENT IRELAND
PLACES OF MYTHOLOGY
IN SEARCH OF DE SELBY
IRISH LANGUAGE IRELAND

Genealogy, History and Memoir
GRANDFATHER'S HOUSE
A WALK ON THE SOUTH SIDE
FRAGMENTS FROM FRESCATI
ATTIC. STUFF. WRITE
CONNECTIONS

Local historical guides to
DALKEY
DÚNLAOGHAIRE
NORTH MAYO
GLASNEVIN CEMETERY
RATHCROGHAN

www.conankennedy.com